W9-DIM-080

# WORLD ECONOMY
# AT THE CROSSROADS

# WORLD ECONOMY
# AT THE CROSSROADS

George Macesich

PRAEGER

**Westport, Connecticut**
**London**

**Library of Congress Cataloging-in-Publication Data**

Macesich, George, 1927–
    World economy at the crossroads / George Macesich.
       p.  cm.
    Includes bibliographical references (p.      ) and index.
    ISBN 0-275-95902-3 (alk. paper)
       1. Economic history—1971–1990.   2. Economic history—1990–
    3. Unemployment—Effect of inflation on.   4. Economic development.
    I. Title.
    HC59.M143   1997
    330.9—dc21          97–19210

British Library Cataloguing in Publication Data is available.

Library of Congress Catalog Card Number: 97–19210
ISBN: 0-275-95902-3

First published in 1997

Praeger Publishers, 88 Post Road West, Westport, CT 06881
An imprint of Greenwood Publishing Group, Inc.

Printed in the United States of America

The paper used in this book complies with the
Permanent Paper Standard issued by the National
Information Standards Organization (Z39.48–1984).

10 9 8 7 6 5 4 3 2 1

*To the Memory*
*of*
*My Uncle*
*George Peter Tepavac*
*1909–1943*

*Killed in Action, World War II*
*June 1943*

# Contents

# Preface

Consider the concern in the economics profession and elsewhere on the apparent collapse of the postwar paradigm. The paradigm apparently foundered on the supposed trade-off between unemployment and inflation.

The increase in both inflation and unemployment as a result of policy manipulation blessed by the paradigm produced consternation in the 1970s and 1980s and search for a substitute paradigm. In the closing years of the twentieth century, the world economy is at a crossroads and the paradigm search continues. This study examines the critical issues underlying this search and the new global political economy that seems to be emerging and replacing the old policy consensus.

The challenge for economists and others is to articulate what in their view constitutes a new paradigm that recognizes the rapid transformation in the late-twentieth-century economy. Not everyone agrees that economics has undergone a Kuhnian paradigm shift. Indeed, the basic paradigm in economics remains as received from Adam Smith more than two hundred years ago. Unlike the case in the physical sciences, the economist's fundamental way of viewing the world remains unchanged. Smith's postulate of the maximizing individual in a relatively free market remains the basic paradigm.

This paradigm can take into account the rapidly growing groups of knowledge workers, who earn their living with their minds, not their muscles. It can also provide insights into the growing worldwide drive for reform and equally unsettling issues that emerge from the rapid globalization of the world economy. And the paradigm can serve as a guide in judging which economies and reforms are likely to succeed and which are likely to fail. Economists and others would do well to study history and understand the discipline of economics in its historical setting. Historical experience is important in economics. In economics, there is no tearing down and reassembling the pieces into something new that qualifies for a Kuhnian paradigm shift.

# 1

# The Problem of Order and Chaos

## A PARADIGM LOST?

From the early post–World War II years to the mid-1970s, there was almost a consensus among economists that economics did indeed possess a "paradigm" capable of dealing with such real-world problems as unemployment, inflation, and monetary policy. In fact, all three are key policy issues.

The "paradigm" at issue is called by economists the "neoclassical" synthesis. Because of serious theoretical and empirical problems, however, this "paradigm"—if we can describe it as such—broke down in the mid-1970s. Attempts by economists to repair it have not been completely successful. The situation is far from hopeless. Economics contains more than two hundred years of experience from which to draw. Indeed, there is good reason for optimism.

The neoclassical synthesis drew from what many economists considered to be both valuable and useful—a combination of both classical and Keynesian economics. The classical contribution was the methodology derived from the propositions that consumers are rational and that markets are such that prices adjust to maintain a balance of supply and demand. To account for the observation that unemployment of resources, which may not be voluntary, does exist and thus is unexplainable in classical economic terms, the "paradigm" drew on the

Keynesian contribution of "sticky prices," which means that prices, and especially wages, move sluggishly.

The paradigm thus proposed that consumers and producers are rational in their pursuit of self-interest and that markets do provide useful insights into the operation of an economy. Keynesians readily accepted the classical view. However, they added to it their own view that slow-changing prices are important to the way an economy behaves, particularly in the short run. Thus, in the long run the economy looks classical, whereas in the short run, if the economy is plagued by unemployment of its resources, the Keynesian description appears more realistic. Putting together the classical long-run view with the Keynesian short-run view yielded the neoclassical synthesis.

The neoclassical paradigm considered the supply side of the economy by zeroing in on the labor market to explain the lack of employment. Together with another equation, which gives an economy's production function, the amount of labor employed would determine the economy's output.

When the Keynesian "sticky wages" contribution is combined within the basic IS-LM framework, the result is the neoclassical paradigm just described. It provides an integrated model of aggregate supply and demand. This is also the basic model that served the construction of the large econometric models of the 1960s, as well as many economic research and policy proposals.

## ORDER OR CHAOS?

During the late 1960s and into the 1970s, econometric models began to produce results that did conform with the neoclassical "paradigm." Increasingly, the users of economic forecasting models based on the neoclassical "paradigm" became more and more skeptical about the forecasts these models produced.

In particular, doubt was cast on the prediction derived from these models—along with the statistical relationship summarized in the Phillips curve—that unemployment went hand in hand with high inflation, and vice versa. As we have noted, the IS-LM framework does provide that a rise in prices could lower real wages, temporarily raising employment and output. Together with the statistical relationship summarized in the Phillips curve, it is possible that rising prices or inflation could boost employment and output. This is the now well-known trade-off between inflation and unemployment, which governments had been urged to watch closely. Any attempts at price stability policy then had to take advantage of the apparent inflation-output trade-off.

It turned out, however, that the trade-off issue was an illusion. In 1968, Milton Friedman looked into its theoretical microeconomic underpinnings, as did Edmond Phelps. The results for the trade-off issue were not encouraging. For the sake of argument, suppose it is true that inflation reduces real wages, and thus the demand for labor increases. The supply of labor may not be as forthcoming if workers are unwilling to supply as much labor as before. As a result, the increased demand for labor may not lead to increased employment. Now, it may be that workers are mistaken about real wages and do not understand that a rise in general prices reduces their real wages and that a stronger demand for labor will increase employment. However, for the Phillips curve to hold, workers must keep making the same mistake. This is highly unlikely. For example, it would mean that if inflation had been averaging 8 percent per year, workers would need to keep on expecting prices to be stable next year; otherwise they would insist on recouping their real wage cut by demanding higher money wages.

This is not a realistic view of the world from the viewpoint of most people. It is not likely that inflation under such circumstances would come as a surprise. For such an event, inflation must be accelerating. There then might indeed be a trade-off between inflation and output. This is likely to be transitory, however, and as people learn to anticipate stable inflation, so too will they learn to anticipate accelerating inflation.

In effect, a Phillips curve exists briefly when people's expectations are upset by surprise. If inflation is fully expected, there is no trade-off between inflation and unemployment. These events are summarized in the now familiar expectations-augmented Phillips curve.

The events of the 1970s, high inflation, and high unemployment— which the former Phillips curve analysis rejected—came as a sobering reality for the neoclassical synthesis. Thus, the postwar "paradigm" collapsed, and with it, its underlying consensus.

## A FALTERING "PARADIGM" OR A DIFFERENT RESEARCH PROGRAM?

Since the 1970s, an economic and political search has gone on for a replacement "paradigm." In the spirit of Friedman's challenge, one group has promoted a view based on the assumption that markets clear. This approach is usually called the New Classical School. Another group has challenged the market-clearing assumption but nonetheless has explored the microeconomic causes of market failure. This group is now called the New Keynesian School.

The breakdown of the postwar consensus has also served to usher in various disputes, some already simmering. Economic forecasting based on a large macroeconometric model has fallen into academic disrepute. Some theorists have been unwilling to cast their ideas in terms of the former "paradigm." Other areas of economics have also come in for new emphasis. Thus, the focus on microeconomic foundations and the emphasis on extremely sophisticated mathematical techniques has brought with it new problems for both economists and politicians. Economists have become less sure of their ability to meet these challenges. Politicians have cast about for a new theoretical edifice on which to hang their programs.

Important elements in this new theoretical edifice, particularly for policy purposes, are the credibility and cooperation of the politicians and bureaucrats responsible for domestic and international economic policies, monetary policy in particular. There is good reason to believe that the interwar consensus on economic policy collapsed from a lack of these two elements, which served to reinforce the neoclassical "paradigm."

It is with good reason that "paradigm" is marked with quotation marks. There are misgivings about Kuhnian methodology applied to economics and the view that "scientific revolutions" characterize the history of economic thought.[1] Recall that Thomas S. Kuhn's thesis is that science is not the steady, cumulative acquisition of knowledge.[2] Instead, Kuhn argues, it is a series of peaceful interludes punctuated by intellectually violent revolutions. In those revolutions, according to Kuhn, one conceptual worldview is replaced by another. In his view, the typical scientist is not an objective freethinker and skeptic. On the contrary, he tends to be a conservative individual who accepts what he is taught and applies his knowledge to solving the problems that came before him (or her).

Accordingly, Kuhn argues that such scientists accept a "paradigm"—an accepted solution to a problem. An example that serves to illustrate a "paradigm" in the Kuhnian sense is Ptolemy's theory that the sun revolves around the earth. Generally conservative, scientists would tend to solve problems in ways that extended the scope of the "paradigm."

During such periods, Kuhn observes, scientists tend to resist research that might signal the development of a new "paradigm," like the work of the astronomer Aristarchus, who theorized in the third century B.C. that the planets revolve around the sun. As Kuhn notes, situations arose that the "paradigm" could not account for or that contradicted it.

It is then, argues Kuhn, that a revolutionary would appear, a Lavoisier or an Einstein, often a young scientist not deeply indoctrinated in the accepted theories, and brush aside the old "paradigm." Such revolutions come only after long periods of tradition-bound science. In effect, frameworks must be lived with and explored before they can be broken. The new "paradigm" cannot build on the one that precedes it. In Kuhn's view, the two are "incommensurable." In essence, the competing paradigms represent not so much two sets of facts and theories as two contradictory ways of seeing the world.

Thus it is that a debate over "paradigms" can never be proved to the point that one of them is right and the other wrong, or that one of them is closer to the truth. Indeed, scientists deliberately, on more than one occasion, choose a "paradigm" for the simple reason that it does not explain everything and thus allows a greater number and variety of puzzles to be solved during the ensuing period of Kuhn's "normal science."

The popularity of Kuhn's ideas is understandable. They do provide scholars with the means to approach the persistent intellectual problem on how ideas develop and change. His ideas provided broader and more realistic definitions of such things as rationality and objectivity. And they came at a time when dissatisfaction with the old notions of science was becoming widespread.

In particular, Kuhn's ideas and view came at the end of an era in which the prevailing view of science was characterized by the "Positivist School" that holds that phenomena are real, certain, and precise, and all knowledge consists in the description of such phenomena. The works of Karl Popper are a case in point. Popper argues that science is a logical exercise consisting in the attempt not to prove theories but to falsify them. That is, the truth of a theory can never be proved beyond doubt. A related view is that science is a cumulative activity in which new facts and theories are added to old ones in an ever closer approximation of the truth. Little wonder that Kuhn's views on how science proceeds created dismay, controversy, and uncertainty among scholars and scientists in many disciplines.

In response to Kuhn's ideas, many scholars argue that these ideas simply will not account for the variety and complexity of how science is conducted. Others argue that Kuhn's definition of "paradigm" is too broad to have any real meaning. Still other scholars accuse Kuhn of the dread sin of relativism. In effect, scientists choose one paradigm over another simply because it seems to fit their current needs.

In reply to the various concerns of scholars, Kuhn insists that he is by no means a relativist. He is prepared to describe criteria by which rational, reasonable, plausible, and well-motivated choices between an older and a newer position can be made. If not a relativist, Kuhn has attracted attention from scholars across the various disciplines. Indeed, in Gutting's collection of essays, the use of the concept of "paradigm" to analyze the evaluation of political theories, history of economics, and other areas is but an illustration. For his part, Kuhn insists that attempts to take his apparatus and apply it simplistically to all fields and disciplines is simply a very poor idea and not very productive.

And indeed, Blaug and others cast doubt that the ruling "paradigm" in the history of economic thought has changed in more than two hundred years. The basic paradigm remains as received from Adam Smith. His postulate of the maximizing individual in a relatively free market remains the basic paradigm. Unlike the case in the physical sciences, the economist's fundamental way of viewing the world has remained unchanged since the eighteenth century.

Blaug notes, however, that if economics provides any examples at all of Kuhnian "scientific revolutions," a number of economists would take as an example the Keynesian Revolution, which has the appearance of a paradigm change. For all his modifications of the received theory from Adam Smith, Keynes nevertheless drew heavily from the concepts of general equilibrium, competition, and comparative statics, taking exception only for the labor market, which he considered inherently imperfect and in a state of equilibrium of a special kind.

To be sure, there are other novel aspects to Keynes's contribution. These include tendencies to work in aggregates, to reduce the economy to three interrelated markets for goods, bonds, and labor; to focus on the short run and to restrict analysis of the long run, which had been the focus of many of his predecessors in observations about secular stagnation; to place emphasis for adjustment on output rather than prices. In sum, equilibrium for the economy in Keynes's view involved "underemployment equilibrium." Keynes, moreover, introduced pervasive uncertainty and the possibility of destabilizing expectations. This is in marked contrast to received theory, which contains the critical idea of rational economic calculation and the existence of certainty equivalents for each uncertain future outcome of current decisions.

For all its apparent novelty, the Keynesian Revolution is more myth than reality. Certainly it is far from a Kuhnian "scientific revolution." Blaug is correct when he writes that it is false to picture a whole generation of economists dumbfounded by the persistence of the Great Depression, unwilling to entertain the obvious remedies of fiscal and monetary policy, unable to find even a language with which to communicate with Keynesians, and finally, in despair, abandoning their old beliefs in a conversion to the new paradigm. The success of Keynesian theory can be attributed more to the fact that at the time it produced a theoretical apparatus for policy conclusions most economists advocated and supported.

It is thus not surprising that Blaug and other economists prefer to talk about "degenerating" and "progressive" research programs that incorporate the ideas of Imre Lakatos. Accordingly, the tendency of economists to join the ranks of the Keynesians in increasing numbers after 1936 simply underscores their switch from a "degenerating" to a "progressive" research program considered more promising in dealing with policy issues of the 1930s.

On this score, the postwar history of Keynesian economics as a progressive research program slipped considerably when the theory's prediction of chronic unemployment failed to materialize. Further doubt is cast on the progressive nature of the Keynesian research program by Milton Friedman's monetarist counterrevolution. The principal tenet of monetarism is that inflation is at all times and everywhere a monetary phenomenon. Its principal policy corollary is that only a slow and steady rate of increase in the money supply—in line with the real growth of the economy—can insure price stability.[3] And indeed, it was inflation in the postwar years that dominated the world scene. As such, it seems that monetarism provides a more "progressive research program," in Blaug's terms.

The monetarist view, as summarized by Friedman in his *Counter-Revolution in Monetary Theory, First Wincott Memorial Lecture* (London: Institute of Economic Affairs, 1970), questions the Keynesian doctrine that variations in government spending, taxes, and the national debt could stabilize both the price level and the real economy. This doctrine has come to be called "the Keynesian Revolution," as we have discussed.

In fact, the battle between Keynesians, neo-Keynesians, and monetarists/quantity-theorists has been waged for decades. It has long since moved into the policy area. The critics of monetarism declare that the proposed monetarist cure for inflation can work only by imposing excessive burdens of huge losses in real output and prolonged output losses on the economy. The monetarists respond that the burden must be borne because there is no other way to restore the economy to price or economic stability.

Critics are quick to point out that monetarism in isolation does not work, as the British and United States experiences show. Its lack of success can be attributed to difficulties at three levels: (1) there is the difficulty as to what is *money*; (2) there is the problem that what a central bank elects to call *money* cannot, either in quantity or velocity, be controlled; (3) there is the certainty that efforts at vigorous control will substitute for the problem of inflation the alternatives of high unemployment, recession or depression, and disaster for those industries that depend on borrowed money. In effect, monetarism, which places its sole confidence in stabilizing the growth of some "esoteric money aggregate" to the exclusion of other concerns, is a prescription for calamity, according to critics.

These critics are distressed that monetarism, which began with the slogan "Money matters" and manifested a healthy skepticism about Keynesian views, has over the years blossomed into all-out opposition to such discretionary Keynesian stabilization policies as compensatory use of fiscal and monetary measures. It is also upsetting to such critics to hear monetarist charges that an active stabilization policy causes more problems than it cures.

Critics charge that monetarists have never really provided a convincing theoretical foundation for their policy prescriptions. There is not, so the critics argue, a clear conceptual basis for a sharp distinction of *money* from its substitutes and for ignoring systematic and random variation in velocity. Apparently, the empirical evidence presented by the monetarists is insufficient.

Monetarists, moreover, are charged by their critics with converting long-run equilibrium conditions into short-run policy recommendations.

Thus, natural rate theory argues that no permanent reduction of unemployment can be gained by accepting inflation. Anti-inflationary policies produce protracted social costs in lost output and unemployment. These costs are not fully addressed by monetarists. This is not surprising, so the critics argue, given their free-market ideology; they will not entertain wage or price controls or income policies as alternatives or complements to anti-inflationary monetary restrictions.

Milton Friedman identifies monetarism with the quantity theory of money, suggesting thereby that monetarism is not a new development. It is also consistent with the quantity theory he freed of dependence on the assumption of automatic full employment, the focal point of Keynesian ridicule of traditional quantity theory. In Friedman's University of Chicago monetary workshop during the 1950s (in which this writer had the privilege of participating as a graduate student), studies on inflation and the role of money in inflation received considerable attention. Friedman's work changed professional thinking on matters pertaining to the role of money.

Harry Johnson has described changes in monetary theory as owing much to Friedman's efforts.[4] Monetary economics is once again exciting and concerned with vital issues, argues Johnson. More fundamentally, the Friedman analysis gives a central place to expectations about future price movements and to Fisher's distinction between real and money rates of interest. This is in marked contrast to Keynesian analysis, which always started with the assumption of stable prices. Friedman's contribution steered theory and empirical research and monetary economics toward concepts and methods far more appropriate to the inflation-cum-recessionary development of the 1960s and 1970s than the concepts and methods Keynesian economics was capable of providing.

It is, in fact, unfair to present Friedman as just another ideologue who lets his politics dominate his economics. Most observers agree that Friedman's political or policy views were, and indeed are, guided by a strong commitment to a relevant empirical use of economic analysis. This has led to a series of quite radical questions bearing on money of our social institutions. Indeed, the proposal for a monetary rule was not motivated by any laissez-faire preconception, but evolved from Friedman's appreciation of the unpredictable variability of monetary lags.[5]

In fact, Keynesian emphasis on the basic instability of the private sector and the stabilizing function of a stable government sector is a

central idea that Brunner correctly notes is turned on its head by Friedman
on the basis of his work with Anna Schwartz on the Great Depression.
Their argument is that it is essentially the stable private sector that
operates as a shock absorber to the shock imposed by an erratic and
unstable government sector. This inversion has generated a considerable
amount of intellectual and political heat.

On each of four of the most important issues in monetary theory,
Friedman has made contributions to our understanding. First is the
impulse problem; second, the nature of the transmission mechanism; third,
the stability of the private sector of the economy; and fourth, the
relevance of allocative detail for the analysis of aggregative behavior.

Concerning the impulse problem, Friedman focused attention on the
need to distinguish between monetary growth and monetary accelerations.
The latter influences employment and output, while the former dominates
the average inflation rate.

On the issue of the transmission mechanism, Friedman's reservations
on the nature and interpretation of the relation between unemployment
and inflation as summarized in the Phillips curve have been borne out by
the worldwide inflationary policies followed in the 1970s. The argument
that a larger inflation could not permanently lower unemployment is now
amply supported by worldwide evidence.

Friedman argues that the dynamic structure of the private sector is
basically stable, absorbing shocks and transforming them into a stabilizing
motion. This is at odds with the traditional Keynesian view, which rests
on the assumption of an inherently unstable economy in which
government activity is designed to offset swings in the level of economic
activity.

Monetarists express little interest in allocative detail in explaining
and predicting short-run changes in income. Since changes in the stock of
money are dominant in explaining changes in nominal income, focus is
placed on the behavior of the market for real cash balances. A sharp
distinction is made between the general level of prices, which is affected
by the quantity of money, and relative prices, which are affected by
particular market conditions in various sectors. This is also the reason for
monetarists' preference for small-scale econometric models. Again, this
is in contrast to Keynesian preferences for large-scale econometric
models, which presumably provide detailed information on various
sectors believed to significantly influence the aggregative behavior of the
economy.

Money and monetary theory has been a matter of concern in the writings of economists for more than two hundred years. It is in this sense, as Friedman observes, that monetarism has a long lineage. Consider the views of the eighteenth- and nineteenth-century economists on the role of money in economic activity.[6] Conditions of economic instability at the beginning of the eighteenth century promoted examination of the connection between money and output. The most outstanding contributors were John Locke (1632–1704) and John Law (1671–1729). In essence, they focused on the obvious fact that total monetary receipts must equal total monetary payments. Locke and Law contended that increases in the quantity of money and in the velocity of circulation not only raised prices, but also expanded output. Their policy prescription was to measure the quantity of money, which included policies designed to create a favorable balance of trade.

Richard Cantillon (1697–1734) focused on the processes by which variations in quantity of money lead to variations in prices and output—thereby providing useful insights into monetary dynamics. He also recognized what many would later point out: that nominal quantity of money is beneficial to trade only during the period in which money is *actually increasing*. Once a new equilibrium is reached, output would return to its original level only with a higher price level. This process of increasing the quantity of money, however, cannot last indefinitely for the reason that the process leads to an adverse balance of payments and so to an outflow of money. How to buy the benefits of the inflationary process without generating balance-of-payments problems is a dilemma all too familiar to contemporary society.

David Hume (1711–1776) and Henry Thornton (1760–1815) draw implications for monetary policy identical to those of Cantillon. Both had little confidence in a policy that would continuously increase the stock of money for any length of time. Ultimately, such a policy would lead to balance-of-payments problems. In effect, Cantillon dealt with money in transition periods, Hume with money in transition periods and comparative equilibria, and Thornton almost exclusively with comparative equilibria.

David Ricardo and John Stuart Mill focused attention on the role of money in comparative statics, due largely to events in the nineteenth century. We have it from other studies that the Industrial Revolution—if one chooses to call the culmination of events and circumstances that occurred in the nineteenth century by this name—did indeed change the economic situation in the 1800s as compared to what went before. Cost reductions, innovations, and movement of money including financial capital, when coupled with the inflation rate during the Napoleonic wars, underscored the importance of "real" forces. Unlike in the eighteenth century, when Cantillon's model appeared most applicable, Ricardo's model in which output is independent of money seemed most appropriate. Mill was straightforward in his argument that the quantity of money was unimportant provided that it was not allowed to get out of order. Economists, however, have been quick to add that money does indeed get out of order, especially during periods when its quantity undergoes rapid change. Indeed, it is the one area into which government intervention (however limited) is allowed by (nineteenth-century) neoliberal doctrine.

To Keynes, writing during the upheaval of the post–World War I period, the nineteenth-century model of Ricardo and Mill offered little in the way of guidance. Money, in fact, was out of order. The uncertainty generated by monetary disturbances affected expectations. People are reluctant to undertake investment in the face of uncertainty generated by such disturbances. If rapid monetary changes have occurred in the past and are expected to be repeated in the future—in which direction no one knows—people will refuse to bear the risk of investment.

Keynes concluded that rapidly fluctuating prices—such as characterized the post–World War I era—would create uncertainty on the part of businesses, which would then reduce the investment so necessary if economic stability was to be achieved. The only recourse, under the circumstances, was for government to undertake the necessary investment. In view of the Bank of England's preoccupation with restoring the pound to prewar gold parity and the willingness to accept and enforce any price fluctuations necessary, Keynes became convinced that Britain would have to place emphasis on means other than monetary policy to stabilize output and prices.

Friedman, too, deplores the uncertainty generated by money disturbances, arguing that marked instability of money is accompanied by instability of economic activity. Keynes and Friedman both desire a stable growth rate in the money supply as a way of minimizing fluctuations in prices, output, and employment. They differ, however, in how they believe we can achieve the benefits of monetary stability. Keynes thought that exclusive reliance on monetary policy was unrealistic on political grounds and opted for fiscal policy. Friedman has little confidence in the role political authorities may play in providing monetary stability, and opts, from both monetary and fiscal authorities, for a fixed rule.

The vexing problem of unemployment with simultaneous inflation received a most explicit and unique examination by Nobel Prize winner F. A. Hayek.[7] His ideas on the possibility of a simultaneous occurrence of unemployment and inflation were put forward in the 1930s, which was not a propitious time for such views. Unemployment so dominated the times that almost no attention was paid to theories purporting to explain the simultaneous occurrence of the two. The 1960s, 1970s, and 1980s, however, are another matter. Keynes's views advanced for the 1930s provide little guidance to contemporary policy makers. But Hayek's views require modifications if they are to be used as aids to understanding the economic scene since 1960.

Hayek's basic theory is that bank credit (or money supply) expansion, by lowering the market rate of interest below the natural rate, benefits private investment at the expense of consumers, owing to a shift of resources for the production of more producer goods. This shift reduces the supply of consumer goods and so raises prices. Consumers are unwilling to pay the now higher prices and so are "freed" to save.

Eventually, the banking system cuts back on its credit advances to producers. If additional savings are not forthcoming, the market rate of interest rises to the natural rate, making additional investment unattractive. Consumer prices, however, continue to advance due to supply reductions and incomplete investment projects that allow nothing to consumer supply. Since workers in the producer goods sector cannot readily shift to the consumer goods sector, the economy is faced with unemployment and rising prices.

Conditions have changed since the 1930s, when Hayek presented his analysis. It is government, not private investment, that benefits by bank credit or money supply increases at the expense of consumers. For example, in the U.S. economy, consumer expenditures as a percentage of GNP declined from 75 percent in 1929 to 63 percent in 1974, whereas government spending increased over the same period from 8 percent to 22 percent. On the other hand, investment, which was 10 percent of GNP in 1929, fell to about 15 percent in 1974.

We should keep in mind that Hayek's views on money and the monetary system are those of the Austrian school and are very close to the views of supply siders who urge a return to the gold standard. Accordingly, money is a social institution—public good. In essence, the monetary system is an integral part of the social fabric whose threads include faith and trust, which make possible the exercise of rational choice and the development of human freedom.

When we turn to the analytical apparatus for examining money, we find that three approaches to monetary analysis have dominated the past few decades: the quantity-velocity approach, the cash-balance approach, and the income-expenditure approach. The Great Depression tended to overshadow the first two approaches, commonly grouped under the quantity theories of money, giving rise to the income-expenditure approach.

The quantity theories, however, have never been completely repudiated. On the contrary, they have experienced a remarkable revival. Closely associated with classical and neoliberal thought, monetarist quantity theories have tended to separate monetary from "real" influences. In interpreting swings in the price level or the value of money, they rest on the assumption, usually implicit, that the structure of relative prices, rates of interest, levels of employment and output, and the rate of economic growth are determined in the long run by "real" (nonmonetary) forces. In this view, the theories of value and distribution explain how the forces of supply and demand determine the relative prices of goods and services. This is accomplished exclusive of money, which is viewed simply as a common unit or measure of account. "Real" forces are, in effect, the important factors underlying economic welfare; money, though useful, is only secondary.

Reform-liberalism and Keynesianism, on the other hand, tend to be associated with the development of the income-expenditure approach. As a result, the traditional separation between monetary and real forces has receded into the background. The scope of monetary theory has broadened so as to take into account the effects of monetary change on real income and employment and the processes of short-run economic adjustments.

Unlike disciplines in the natural sciences, economics does not suffer from "paradigm" shifts in the Kuhnian sense. Thanks to its anchor in the social sciences and humanities, a more useful approach to problems confronted in the discipline is to draw for assistance and insight into its accumulated knowledge over the past centuries. To be sure, Kuhn's work has stimulated many attempts by social scientists, particularly economists and sociologists, to give "Kuhnian" accounts of the history and current status of their disciplines.

## NOTES

1. For instance, see Mark Blaug, "Kuhn versus Lakatos, or Paradigm versus Research Programmes in the History of Economics," in *Paradigms and Revolutions*, ed. Gary Gutting (Notre Dame, IN: University of Notre Dame Press, 1980), pp. 137–59.

2. Thomas S. Kuhn, *The Structure of Scientific Revolutions*, second edition, enlarged (Chicago: University of Chicago Press, 1970).

3. "I must say that personally I do not like the term *monetarism*," writes Friedman. "I would prefer to talk simply about the quantity theory of money, but we can't avoid usage that custom imposes on us." Milton Friedman, "Monetary Policy: Theory and Practice," *Journal of Money, Credit, and Banking* (February 1982), p. 101. For a discussion of monetarism, see George Macesich, *Monetarism: Theory and Policy* (New York: Praeger, 1983).

4. Harry Johnson, "The Nobel Milton," *The Economist*, October 23, 1976, p. 95.

5. Karl Brunner, "The 1976 Nobel Prize in Economics," *Science*, November 5, 1976, p. 648.

6. In some of the early writers, we see anticipations of theories advanced much later, for example, Thomas Joplin (1790–1847), Thomas Attwood (1783–1856), Nicholas Barbour (1640–1698), William Lowndes (1652–1724), and Bishop George Berkeley (1658–1753). D. Vickers, *Studies in the Theory of Money, 1690–1776* (Philadelphia: Chilton, 1959) makes the point that there was more Keynesian-type economics in the early period than has often been recognized.

7. F. A. Hayek, *The Constitution of Liberty* (Chicago: University of Chicago Press, 1960).

# 2

## Money and Inflation

### INFLATION: A MONETARY PHENOMENON

Critical to discussion of "paradigms" or different research programs is the relation between money and inflation. The relation is indeed close. On this score little if anything has changed over the years to shake our confidence. Inflation continues to be a monetary phenomenon.

According to some economists and other observers, inflation that once ravaged world economies in the 1970s and 1980s is in the 1990s a dead issue. In effect, countries can now enjoy inflation-free growth. Moreover, such growth can be rapid, if respective monetary authorities and central banks would only ease up and stop fighting past battles.

To be sure, inflation in the leading seven industrial economies has been lower than many people expected. In 1996, the average rate of inflation (rise in the general level of prices) has been a relatively modest 2.3 percent, which is close to a thirty-year low. Globalization and increased international and technological change may well be responsible, as some analysts argue. It would be wrong, however, to believe that inflation has, in fact, been defeated. Indeed, bond markets certainly do not believe that inflation is no longer a problem. This concern is indicated by yields on thirty-year American bonds that are close to 7 percent, suggesting that investors expect future inflation to average 3 to 4 percent.

Many of the same factors that are underscored and cited by analysts who insist that inflation is yesterday's battle were also with us in the past. Thus, technological change was just as rapid in the 1980s as it is in the 1990s. Imports from low-wage countries are not much bigger in the 1990s than they were in the 1980s. Neither factor prevented inflation from taking off in a number of the industrial countries. Whatever the merits of the argument that official price indexes overstate the true rate of inflation, in many countries such assurances provide little guarantee that inflation will not revive.

Inflation is, after all, a monetary phenomenon. It is the result of too much money chasing too few goods. Countries that pursue sound money and fiscal policies also have lower rates of inflation. It is these sound policies, and not technology and globalization, that leave inflation low in most industrial countries. Monetary authorities, including central banks, would do well to consider that fighting inflation is a never-ending task.

Milton Friedman's famous proposition that inflation is always and everywhere a monetary phenomenon continues as a sound policy guide. The source of all inflations, in his view, is a high rate of growth of the money supply. Inflation can be prevented simply by reducing the growth rate of the money supply to low levels. Certainly, such action will prevent the inflationary fire from igniting. To be sure, inflationary monetary policy is an offshoot of other government policies: the attempt to hit high employment targets or the running of large budget deficits.

The evidence for Friedman's observation is considerable. In every instance in which a country's inflation rate is extremely high for any sustained period of time, its rate of money supply growth is extremely high.

In the 1970s to the mid-1980s, the inflation experienced by various Latin American countries can, in many of their cases, be attributed directly to the growth rates of their money supplies. Indeed, countries with very high inflation also have the highest rates of money growth. In some of the Latin American countries, a third factor that drives both inflation and money growth could be operating. A case in point could well be their unstable political systems.

We do have other historical examples in which increases in money growth appear to be exogenous. Hyperinflations do indeed exist, and we have examples. One of the most famous examples is the German hyperinflation in 1921–1923. Following World War I, Germany's need to make reparation payments and reconstruct the economy caused government expenditures to greatly exceed revenues. Of course, the German government could have increased taxes so as to raise the necessary revenues. This was certainly politically unpopular. And in any case, such a course of action would have taken time. Borrowing from the public could have produced some revenue, but probably not enough to meet the German government's needs. The one sure route left for it was to resort to the printing press. The government could pay for its expenditures simply by printing more currency. In effect, by increasing the money supply, the government could make payments to those people that were providing it with goods and services. And of course, this is exactly what the German government did. By 1921, the German money supply began to grow rapidly, and so did the price level.

By 1923, the German government's budgetary situation deteriorated even further. When the Germans were unable to make further reparation payments, the French occupied the Ruhr. A general strike of protest against the French action by German workers resulted. The German government supported the strikers by making payments to them. One consequence was that the German government's expenditures increased dramatically, and the government printed currency at an even faster rate to finance the increased spending. The result of the explosion in the German money supply produced an inflation for 1923 that exceeded 1,000,000 percent.

Certainly a third factor that could have driven both inflation and money growth did not exist in the German example. It would be nonsense to argue that the price level caused the French to occupy the Ruhr, which is what reverse causation would require. The German example does fit the characteristics of an exogenous event. It is in support of Friedman's proposition that inflation is a monetary phenomenon.

Other examples, if perhaps not as dramatic as the German experience, are provided by Argentina and Brazil in the decade from 1977 to 1987. Both countries had the highest rates of money growth and the highest average inflation rates. The explanation for the high rate of money growth is similar to the explanation for Germany during its hyperinflation. Both Argentina and Brazil were unwilling (or unable for political reasons) to finance their government expenditures by raising taxes to cover large budget deficits. They both turned to the printing press, with predictable results. Their experience supports the proposition that high money growth causes inflation.

Phillip Cagan, in a major study of seven hyperinflations following two world wars, reaches a similar conclusion.[1] Large increases in the supply of money produced large increases in the general level of prices. The reason for the large increase in money is simply that its issue serves as a major source of funds for government expenditures, as Cagan underscores. The inflation resulting from the new increases in money serves as a tax on cash balances by depreciating the value of money.

## INFLATION AS A METHOD FOR RAISING REVENUE

For all practical purposes, inflation is, as Cagan discusses, a method for raising revenues by a special kind of tax and so is particularly attractive to government. This is a tax on the real money holdings or, in the technical jargon of the economist, on the real cash balances.

When a government is either too weak or is unwilling on grounds of political expediency to enact adequate tax programs and to administer them effectively, it resorts to inflation as a method of raising revenue. This tax is often appealing because it does not require detailed legislation and can be administered very simply. All that is required is to spend the newly created money. The resulting inflation automatically imposes a tax on the real money holdings or cash balances of individuals. The tax rate is the rate of depreciation in the real value of money, which is equal to the rate of rise in prices. The revenue (in real terms) is the product of this base and the rate. The money-issuing authorities "collect" all the revenue. When prices rise in greater proportion than the quantity of money, that is, when the real value of cash balances declines, part of the revenue goes to reduce the real value of the outstanding money supply. At the same time, inflation also reduces the real value of the principal and interest charges of debt fixed in money or nominal terms. Thus, total revenue for a period of time is the sum of two factors: first, the real value of new money issued per period of time; and second, the reduction in outstanding monetary liabilities, equal to the decline per period of time in the real value of cash balances. It should be noted, however, that the money-issuing authorities do not set the tax rate directly. They set the rate at which they increase the money supply, and this rate determines the tax rate through the willingness of individuals to hold and not spend the additional money supply.

Institutions other than the government have money-issuing powers. Insofar as these institutions exercise these powers, they share in some of the revenue from the tax, even though the initiating factor is government creation of money. However, in past inflations these other institutions, for the most part, largely dissipated the revenue from their share of the tax. Banks, for example, largely dissipated their share by making loans at minimal rates of interest that did not take full account of the subsequent rise in prices. Thus the real rate of interest received was in the average below the real return that could be obtained on capital. The revenue dissipated went to the borrowers.

The revenue received by the government consequently depends on the tax base, the tax rate, and the fraction of the revenue that goes either to institutions such as banks or to their borrowers. However, a higher tax rate will not yield a proportionally higher revenue because the tax base, or the level of real cash balances, will decline in response to a higher rate. As an increasing number of people begin to believe in the inevitableness of inflation, their money holdings will ultimately decline more than in proportion to the rise in tax rate, so that a higher rate will yield less revenue. It is at this point that inflation enters into a transition between "creeping" and "galloping" varieties.

Phillip Cagan examines the productivity of taxation through inflation. He finds that the actual share of national income procured for different governments that used inflation as a means of taxation was 3 to about 15 percent, except in Imperial Russia, which had an unusually low percentage of 0.5.[2] In almost all cases, the revenue collected by the inflationary tax was lower on the average than could have been collected by other means of taxation, given that the respective countries had a stable growth in the money supply.

## BUDGET DEFICITS AND EMPLOYMENT GOALS

The inflation of the 1960s and early 1970s can be readily traced to the worldwide rate of monetary expansion. The United States in particular played a critical role in the inflation. In fact, the monetary expansion originated in the United States and in its budget deficits, which resulted from the attempt to finance the Vietnam War without tax increases. This was accentuated, moreover, on a worldwide basis by the once and for all phenomenon of the development of the Eurodollar market, where the American balance-of-payments deficit provided a reserve base for the creation of further additions to the world money supply.

Clearly, budget deficits are an important source of inflationary monetary policy. Received theory argues a government can finance its budget deficits in either one of two ways: by selling bonds to the public, or by money creation, in effect, printing money. Selling bonds to the public has no direct effect on the money base and so on the money supply. Creating or printing money, however, does impact on a country's aggregate demand and can create inflation.

For inflation to develop, we have noted that the money supply must grow continually. A budget deficit that persists over a significant period of time can be financed by money creation and so increase the money supply. If in the subsequent periods of time the budget deficits persist and are financed by printing more money, the money supply will increase and continue to do so as long as the process is continued. In sum, a deficit can indeed be a source of persistent and sustained inflation, provided it is persistent and not temporary and the government resorts to printing money rather than issuing bonds.

Not every country has a well established and efficient capital market where government bonds can be readily sold. In many emerging market economies, issuing bonds is not a practical solution for the government. Typically, these governments resort to printing money to cover their deficits. When they continue to run large deficits relative to their Gross National Product (GNP), the money supply will continue to grow and so will inflation.

In the United States, neither access to capital markets by the government nor the underdeveloped nature of these markets describes the situation in the country. Indeed, the American government-bond market is the best developed in the world. The country can and does issue large quantities of bonds to finance deficits that, by comparison to other countries and relative to GNP, are small. Nonetheless, persistent deficits in the United States can ultimately lead to inflation if the Federal Reserve continues to purchase bonds to cover such deficits. The net effect of the Federal Reserve's open market purchases of government bonds issued for the purpose of financing the deficit will lead to an increase in high-powered money and in the money supply, and so in inflation, if continued. Fortunately, American experience with budget deficits as a source of inflation does not appear significant.

One goal that most governments pursue and that results in inflation is high employment. Most governments are committed by law to promoting high employment. In the United States, the Employment Act of 1946 and the Humphrey-Hawkins Act of 1978 are cases in point. In theory, both laws require a commitment to high employment that is consistent with a stable general level of prices. In practice, in the 1960s and 1970s, the American government, in common with other governments, had pursued a target of a high level of employment without too much concern about the inflationary consequences of such a policy. These policies may well have changed in the 1990s.

## ATTACHING LABELS TO INFLATION: HOW USEFUL?

Activist and interventionist government policies to promote high employment can produce and indeed have produced inflation. In fact, economic literature and the popular press have presented two ways that the goal of high employment can lead to inflationary monetary policy. One is the so-called cost-push inflation, which occurs because of the push by workers to get higher wages or firms' attempts to get higher prices. The other is demand-pull inflation, which occurs as policy makers attempt to increase aggregate demand (i.e., shift out the aggregate demand curve in the economy).[3]

It is generally agreed that many of the inflation theories of the cost-push varieties are in the Keynesian tradition. A common thread is the assertion that the pricing mechanism is becoming progressively less sensitive. Whatever the alleged cause of inflation, the monetary preconditions must be satisfied so that the distinction among theories in the Keynesian tradition is between different mechanisms of inflation. Three variations on the theme, however, appear sufficiently important from a public policy viewpoint to warrant consideration. One is that union pressures for wage increases are the causal element in inflation. The second is that oligopolistic sectors administer prices and so are the causal element in inflation. The third incorporates elements of the first two and tangentially places the blame for inflation on the existence of both unions and oligopolistic industries.

The first variation argues that unions are responsible for inflation in that they fail to recognize that wage increases that go beyond overall productivity gains are inconsistent with stable prices. Thus the argument is that unions push up wages, which raises costs and prices. In order to avoid a logical fallacy, the more sophisticated argue that since the monetary authorities are committed to a policy of full employment, they will expand the money supply so as to make possible the sale of the old output at the new price level.

The second variation argues that prices are set in a different way in those sectors of the economy that are composed of many firms than they are in industries where there are few major producers. Prices set by oligopolistic industries are administered so that they are excellent conductors of inflationary pressure. They are relatively immune to traditional anti-inflationary policies in that their prices, having once reached a high level, are stickier in declining than those of competitive industries when demand declines.

The third variation claims that both unions and oligopolistic industries are primarily responsible for inflation. Unions, so the argument goes, lodge themselves in oligopolistic industries and share in the spoils derived from the product ride. Thus, unions in such industries may take advantage of the inelastic or expanding demand conditions on the product market to obtain higher wages without fear that the entry of new firms will reduce union wage gains. According to this variation, the product market permitting, the oligopolist will grant a higher wage rate as a means of avoiding a more costly strike. Moreover, in contradiction to more traditional views, such unions need not be old craft unions; they may be the new industrial unions that economists have tended to treat as relatively powerless in setting excessive wages. It is for this reason, presumably, that the advent of new industrial unions, when coupled with oligopolistic industries, has changed the American economic system so greatly as to largely frustrate attempts to control inflation along traditional lines. In effect, the argument implicitly assumes that the pricing mechanism is becoming progressively less fluid or "automatic."

In place of traditional methods for coping with inflation, which some Keynesians consider largely ineffective or inappropriate, they advocate a direct assault on the problem of inflation. Although such an assault may take may forms, three seem to be dominant. First, government should resort to "moral suasion" to induce business and labor to exercise their power in a socially desirable (noninflationary) way. Second, government could increase the degree of competition in the marketplace by a more vigorous enforcement of antitrust legislation. Some people argue that since labor unions are monopolies, they should also be subject to antitrust legislation. Third, government can participate more actively in or control the price-and-wage-setting process. Needless to say, these forms of control are not mutually exclusive.

Eclectics view the discussion of whether inflation is demand-pulled or cost-pushed as analogous to "Which came first, the chicken or the egg?" They attempt to synthesize, in varying degrees of sophistication, the two views of inflation. Of the several syntheses available, we shall consider only two. One, which draws heavily from the Keynesian tradition, turns on the assertion that we cannot empirically isolate inflation by types. The other, which draws heavily from the quantity-theory monetarist tradition, asserts that we cannot conceptually isolate inflation by types.

The synthesis that draws heavily from the Keynesian tradition asserts that it is impossible empirically to test for the existence of leads or lags from the cost or demand side, which is necessary if we are to classify inflation by types. For such a purpose, we need minute data on the cost and demand sides. Since such data presumably are not available, we cannot meaningfully classify inflation by types.

Even if such data were available, they would shed little light on the causes of inflation. Prices and wages, according to this view, are not set in the traditional manner. They are set with reference to some markup over the cost of living. Accordingly, inflation is generated whenever labor and management attempt to get more than 100 percent of the selling price. This is an impossible situation. Yet it is on the very impossibility of the situation that the continuing process of inflation depends. Thus each party increases the part he tries to take by increasing wages or increasing prices. Since together they cannot succeed in getting more than 100 percent of the selling price, wages and prices are continually raised, thereby generating a continuing process of inflation. The process of inflation, though it may originate in the noncompetitive sector, where market power is sufficient to raise prices and wages, will spill over into the competitive sectors, thereby gaining momentum.

This may occur, it is argued, from the demand side, the cost side, or both. Since the prices of the products and services of the noncompetitive sector rise, there will be a change in the composition of demand. Consumers will switch their demand to the products and services produced by the competitive sector so that prices rise in this sector. There is excess demand in the competitive sector and a deficiency of demand in the noncompetitive sector. The deficiency of demand will result in some unemployment in the noncompetitive sector. Owing to factor immobility, however, unemployment in this sector will not cause prices or wages to fall, so that unemployment persists. Attempts by the government to remove excess demand along traditional lines so as to check the overall price rise, while removing excess demand in the competitive sector, increases still further the unemployment in the noncompetitive sector. The same situation will prevail even if the spillover occurs from the cost side. Thus the spillover will occur because wage or price rises in the noncompetitive sector are signals for labor and employers in the competitive sector to do the same in order to protect, if not increase, their relative income shares. Accordingly, the government is confronted with the dilemma of either inflation or unemployment.

The other view, which borrows heavily from the traditional position, argues that we cannot even conceptually identify inflation by types, much less classify them empirically. In essence, this view turns on the proposition that while it is obvious that demand conditions influence costs, it is equally obvious that one cannot separate out the portion of the cost increase attributable to increased demand. Traditional monetarists and Keynesians accordingly have erred in attempting to establish rigid links between types of inflation and public policy.

The eclectic views essentially do not consider as practical the argument that the monetary authority, by refusing to expand the money supply, could "nip in the bud" an inflationary spiral. The bases for such an assertion are, first, that velocity would increase, thereby frustrating the efforts of the monetary authority, and second, even if velocity could no longer increase, the monetary authority could overcome the strong institutional forces making for rigidity in the pricing system only at the expense of a possible serious depression.

In order to control inflation, therefore, steps should be taken to remove institutional and other rigidities from the American economic system. It is only then that the control of inflation along more traditional lines would have effect.

We may now turn to an appraisal of these views of inflation by drawing on both economic theory and recent experience. Theoretical and empirical evidence, though not completely inconsistent with alternative views, tends to support traditional monetarists' views of inflation.

The fundamental discovery of those de-emphasizing the traditional view of inflation is that prices and wages go up when somebody raises them. There is general agreement as to the facts. We take it to be true that most sellers would always like to raise their prices. We take it to be true that sellers will never raise their prices without limit. What are the limits and circumstances under which sellers will raise their prices? It is precisely to the answering of this question that economists have directed their labors.

The fruit of this labor has produced the consensus that the state of demand will set the limit and circumstances under which sellers can raise or lower prices. The state of demand permitting, sellers can raise their prices without being penalized by a loss of sales and income, and so they decide to raise prices. If, on the other hand, the state of demand permits a rise in prices only at the expense of losing net income, sellers will not raise prices. There is thus no conflict between the view that prices rise because somebody raises them and the view that somebody decides to raise prices because the state of demand permits such a rise without losing sales and income.

The views that de-emphasize the traditional approach to inflation do not provide an alternative theory of inflation that is independent of the state of demand. Although not new, they gained currency in the post–World War II period, when a favorable state of demand was assured by the existence of large liquid asset holdings by individuals and firms. The assurance of a favorable state of demand permitted price increases without the loss of incomes, and so sellers decided to raise prices. In effect, the decision to raise prices is simply the form whereby a disequilibrium situation was brought into balance. In the absence of a favorable state of demand, however, such a decision may result in distortions in the relative price structure, or a one-time increase in the general level of prices coupled with a loss of sales and increased unemployment. There is nothing in the process whereby sellers decide to raise prices that will assure a favorable state of demand. It is essentially for this reason that these views have descriptive but not analytical validity.

Consider the view that unions are responsible for inflation in that they push up wages. In support of this view, evidence is presented that unit labor costs (in money forms) have risen faster than productivity. Needless to say, in a period of inflation, this observation is a truism. It does not help us to tell whether wages pushed up prices or demand pulled up wages.

Studies have underscored that in the absence of a favorable state of demand, unions can cause either shifts in the relative wage structure or a one-time increase in the general level of wages together with increased unemployment.[4] The flexibility of minimum wages determines what will actually occur. On the other hand, if the state of demand is favorable, union wage increases can be followed by inflation and continued full employment.

An important but unfortunately neglected point is that a necessary (but not sufficient) condition for unions to set off a wage-price spiral is that they need more than power to raise wages: they must have increasing power to do so. Indeed, this is a point stressed by Milton Friedman in 1959.[5] There is little serious scholarly evidence to substantiate the view that unions are becoming increasingly strong. Indeed, to judge from the size of union membership roles and recent unfavorable legislation, that power may be decreasing.

The limitations just mentioned similarly restrict the usefulness of the eclectic view that inflation is triggered and generated whenever labor and management attempt to get more than 100 percent of the selling price. It too depends on the existence or assurance of a favorable state of demand. At the same time, each party must be increasing its power as a necessary condition for setting off the wage-price spiral.

The positions that argue that union demands spill over into competitive sectors and so cause wages and firms to rise in this sector also depend, contrary to many of their adherents, on the existence of a favorable state of demand. This state of demand occurs when union employers bid away more and better workers from other employers, and so lead these employers to raise wages in order to hold their employees. Again, there is no conflict between the view that wages and prices rise because somebody raises them and the view that somebody raises them because a favorable state of demand for such a rise exists.

If the state of demand is not favorable to such a rise, a very different story will unfold and we may just as well talk in turns of a "spill-in" effect (movement of labor from union to nonunion activities). If, owing to higher wages, union employers curtail employment, the movement of general wages will depend upon two conditions. First, if wages elsewhere are flexible downward, the union workers will spill into nonunion activities, and so nonunion wages will tend to fall. The movement in the general level of wages, if any, will depend on the precise shapes of demand schedules of union and nonunion employers. Second, if wages elsewhere are not flexible downward, the general wage level will rise but the resulting unemployment will check any further rise. Under these circumstances, nonunion employers are very unlikely to repeat the wage-rise experiment of union employers.

Consider now the view that oligopolies and monopolies, by administering prices, cause inflation. As noted previously, the assertion is that administered prices are more rigid than competitive prices, and so are excellent conductors of inflation.

It has been long noted, however, that administered prices are not as rigid as they seem.[6] Insofar as these prices are rigid, their role in inflation is misunderstood. According to the interpretation, administered prices during periods when the state of demand is favorable do not rise as rapidly as competitive prices, so in effect, they may well be below levels that would clear the market, thereby creating waiting lists and grey markets. When administered prices do rise, however, they are apt to do so in large jumps, thereby attracting widespread attention and charges that they are responsible for inflation.

The reverse argument—that administered prices are rigid in the downward side and so respond more slowly to an unfavorable state of demand than competitive prices—also leaves much to be desired. In the first instance, the evidence used to support this assertion is far from conclusive. Thus the usual evidence cited is that after World War II, during periods when the state of demand was unfavorable, output and employment declined but prices, as judged by price indexes, did not. An examination of the past record suggests that this is not a unique experience. In almost half the recessions since 1920, the consumer index rose in the early months. Moreover, these price indexes, among other limitations, do not pick up price changes that take the form of special discounts or other informal price concessions, such as freight absorption or advertising allowances. The effect is an understatement of actual price changes, and so overstates the actual degree of rigidity. In the second instance, it should be noted that insofar as the administered price argument throws the blame for inflation on large corporations, available studies suggest little if any relation between concentration ratios and price rigidity.

In the view of money economists, the source of price rigidity is not the market sector of the economy but, ironically, the government sector. It is this sector that administers rigid prices through the medium of various regulatory agencies, price support programs, minimum wages, agricultural marketing programs, and support of restrictions on both domestic and foreign trade. Such policies are largely inconsistent with attempts to remove monopoly elements from the economy.

According to the view that incorporates unions on the factor side and oligopolies on the product side, large wage increases won by strategically placed unions may lead to (1) distortion of the wage structure if other wages lag, or (2) rising costs and upward pressure on prices if other wages rise equivalently, or a combination of the two. The net effect will be that the economy will move between episodes of price plateaus (accompanied by a stretching of the wage structure) succeeded by periods of rising prices.

But this view, as with others that de-emphasize the traditional approach to inflation, contributes nothing essentially new to our understanding of inflation. The traditional view does not levy that unions may "distort" wages or that unions may share in monopoly spoils. As noted elsewhere, in the absence of a favorable state of demand, this may be over the effects of a union wage rise. As the view under discussion claims, the precise proportion between wage-distorting and cost-inflationary forces depends upon the economic climate—in particular upon the level of national income. It simply reasserts the traditional view, with its emphasis on the favorable state of demand.

The interesting point about this view is the implicit assertion that new industrial unions and oligopolies have, apparently, sufficiently changed the economic structure so that the pricing system lacks fluidity. Little evidence other than casual empiricism is offered in support of the view. Indeed, such evidence as we do have supports the opposite view—that the pricing mechanism is not becoming progressively less sensitive.

Some consider the distinction between demand-pull and cost-push inflation useless. One view is that we cannot empirically identify inflation by types. This view apparently turns on the question of the timing of demand-pull and cost-push types of inflation; that is, on the identification of the lead and lag series. If the inflation is of the demand-pull type, then presumably demand should lead the increase in costs. If it is cost-push, then costs should lead demand.

To put the distinction between the two types of inflation in this manner is to hopelessly confuse the issue. One would be hard put indeed to identify the existence of leads and lags in the various relevant series. The consensus, however, seems to be that the essential difference between the two types of inflation is to be found not in the timing of the various series, but rather in their sensitivity to changes in demand.

Thus, if the struggle to obtain more than 100 percent of the selling price is sensitive to sales losses and unemployment, then it is very unlikely that the struggle will continue in observance of a favorable state of demand. On the other hand, if in the face of an unfavorable state of demand, the struggle is such that substantial losses in sales and unemployment are the consequence, it does make sense to talk in terms of types of inflation.

Another view is that we cannot even conceptually classify inflation by type. This view is interesting in that at times it is similar to the argument that raged in the latter part of the nineteenth century over the determination of value. The view states that we cannot identify that part of the price rise attributed to a cost increase and that part attributed to an increase in demand. The argument was settled, of course, when it occurred to economists that "each blade in a pair of scissors cuts." The analogy between the controversies breaks down because this view claims too much. Economists have long held that although each blade cuts, it makes sense to distinguish between the blades. Changes in the price level may occur with shifts in the supply schedules or the demand schedules or both.

To argue that we cannot conceptually identify which part of a price rise is attributed to costs and which demand is to assert that we are always in a position whereby both schedules shift simultaneously and by the same amount. It would not be difficult to conjure up cases in which either demand or supply is the dominant element in price rises.

Although arguments against traditional methods of controlling inflation take many forms, they do possess a common thread: we cannot expect high levels of employment and output and at the same time maintain stability in the general level of prices. This is now the familiar unemployment versus inflation dilemma. Owing to the lack of fluidity in our pricing system, we cannot, so the argument goes, attempt seriously to use traditional methods against inflation because their use would simply add to unemployment. Inflation, accordingly, is the necessary price we must pay for avoiding unemployment and, presumably, for maintaining high levels of output.

This represents another aspect of inflation views drawing on the Keynesian tradition. It attempts to rationalize the relation of wage and price movements to aggregate demand and supply through the Phillips curve, which argues a link between variations in employment (capacity utilization) and price changes. A critical question for this analysis is whether adjustments are made in money or real terms. The Phillips curve analysis is discussed at some length by Milton Friedman.[7]

**NOTES**

1.    Phillip Cagan, "The Monetary Dynamics of Hyperinflation," in *Studies in the Quantity Theory of Money*, ed. Milton Friedman (Chicago: University of Chicago Press, 1956), pp. 25–117.

2.    Ibid., pp. 25–117. See also Milton Friedman, "Government Revenue from Inflation," *Journal of Political Economy* (July/August 1971), especially pp. 852–54.

3.    For a discussion of the various types of inflation, see George Macesich, *Monetarism: Theory and Policy* (New York: Praeger, 1983), pp. 139–58.

4.    See Albert Rees, "Do Unions Cause Inflation?" *Journal of Law and Economics* (October 1959), pp. 84–94.

5.    See Milton Friedman, "Current Critical Issues in Wage Theory and Prices," in *Proceedings of the Eleventh Annual Meeting*, Industial Relations Research Association (Chicago, 1959).

6.    For example, see Martin J. Bailey, "Administered Prices and Inflation," in U.S. Congress, Joint Economic Committee, *The Relationship of Prices to Economic Stability and Growth, Compendium*, March 1958.

7.    Milton Friedman. "The Role of Monetary Policy." *American Economic Review* 58 (March 1968), pp. 1–17.

# 3

## The Monetary and Financial Organization

### UNRESOLVED ISSUE

Innovations in the monetary financial framework are regarded by some observers as instances of revolutions in economics. Whether in fact these changes are or can be considered revolutionary remains largely a matter of opinion. Changes that we would call significant and important have occurred in the monetary and financial framework both in theory and in practice. This has been the case since the Great Depression of the 1930s and for a good part of the post–World War II period. Nevertheless, the fundamental problem for policy makers remains. In effect, how much discretion ought to be granted to the monetary authorities? This chapter considers the unresolved issues of discretion and rules in the debate over monetary policy.

### INFLUENCE OF MONETARY AUTHORITIES

The influence of monetary authorities through central bank operations has changed markedly from even so recent a period as the 1970s and 1980s. The so-called transmission mechanism of the 1990s through which monetary policy influences the general economy is but a case in point. For instance, the Federal Reserve System (Fed) has the most influence over short-term interest rates through its federal funds rate. This is the rate that banks pay each other for overnight borrowing. Thus the Fed announces a target federal funds rate and then influences movements in this rate by buying government securities from, or selling them to, banks. A higher federal funds rate promotes a rise in other short-term interest rates as banks pass their increased funding costs on to their customers.

The standard explanation argues that as the nominal interest rate rises but people's expectations of inflation stay the same, real interest rates will rise. The effect is an increase in the cost of borrowing and the return on savings and thus a fall in consumption and investment. The economy slows down and inflationary pressure is eased.

Another channel through which monetary policy operates is the wealth effect. In this instance higher interest rates mean that future revenue from such assets as equities must be discounted at a higher than earlier rate. As a consequence, the holders of such assets now feel poorer and so spend less. At the same time, a fall in the market value of existing firms makes it relatively less expensive to acquire new assets by buying existing firms rather than buying new equipment. The net result is to lower investment expenditures.

Exchange rates are also influenced by changes in interest rates. Thus, a rise in interest rates, other things equal, will tend to appreciate a country's currency. On balance, the appreciating-currency country will find its exports more expensive and its imports less expensive, resulting in a slowdown in domestic output.

Other observers cite bank practices that can be altered by central bank actions. For instance, banks may well respond to a tighter monetary policy by raising their loan rates while at the same time reducing the number of their loans.

It is the financial markets, however, that have gained recently in significance as a channel through which monetary policy operates. Central bank operations do indeed alter financial market expectations about future inflation rates. The financial markets may well be convinced by central bank action to raise short-term rates that the bank is serious about controlling inflation and so limit any increase in long-term rates. Given that bond yields, for instance, adjust very quickly to financial and other sensitive runs, capital markets can more rapidly reinforce central bank action than ordinary banks.

This relationship between financial markets and central banks, however, rests on the central bank's credibility on resolutely controlling inflation. In effect, a central bank with credibility and a strong anti-inflationary record can cut financial market expectations regarding inflation much quicker and so squeeze inflation at a smaller cost in terms of the economy's output and unemployment. Central bank credibility is the basic ingredient for carrying out a successful policy of controlling inflation.

Indeed, in the 1990s inflation in the industrial countries has averaged 3.5 percent, compared with 6 percent a year in the 1980s.[1] Long-term rates have fallen as well, from 10 percent to 7.2 percent. Expectations of inflation have gone down. At the same time, the credibility of many central banks as inflation tightens has increased. Clearly, if central banks and monetary authorities can preserve their credibility as inflation fighters, their policies may well work quicker, thanks to the growing influence of financial markets in shaping the effect of monetary policy.

Various countries have experienced different impacts in their monetary policy channels. For instance, in the United States, Germany, and Italy, the effect on banks' lending rates of a one-percentage-point rise in official short-term interest rates fell fairly sharply between 1975–1989 and 1990–1996, which suggests that the traditional transmission mechanism has lost some of its force.[2] Japan and Canada, on the other hand, register a modest rise.

Other evidence suggests that stock market capitalization has grown far faster than banks' liabilities, measured by broad-money aggregates in, for example, the United States, Sweden, and France. An implication of such a development is that in these three countries, banks have become less important conductors of monetary policy. In Japan, however, the importance of banks in the transmission mechanism has risen. In a number of European countries the relative importance of banking has remained constant.

It may be that the relative effectiveness of monetary channels is changing; monetary policy, however, has lost none of its overall potency.[3] Indeed, for many countries for which results are available, a rise in short-term interest rates has a stronger and quicker effect on output in the 1990s than it did in the 1970s and 1980s. Again, the growing importance of financial markets in shaping the effect of monetary policy is growing. An important result is that central bankers can expect that their policies may well work faster in the future, provided that they can achieve and preserve credibility in preserving price stability and so controlling inflation.

## THE ISSUE OF CREDIBILITY

The issue of credibility of central banks and monetary authorities is indeed critical. Some observers argue that the monetary authorities actually limit the scope of their discretion by adhering to a fairly restrictive rule or set of rules governing the determination of the money supply. Indeed, the type of behavior necessary to convince the public of the authorities' determination could most likely resemble a nondiscretionary path. The fact is that a major difficulty in designing an optimal monetary arrangement is that we do not know enough about the rate at which the credibility of monetary authorities is eroded by the exercise of discretionary power.

Concern over the credibility of monetary authorities has prompted recent examinations of the history of the gold standard and proposals that the United States return to such a standard.[4] The appeal of the gold standard is its presumed tendency toward a predictable long-run value of the monetary unit. Under the gold standard, the United States government is committed to keeping the price of gold fixed and is willing to convert the dollar into gold at a fixed price. Such an arrangement requires the Treasury to maintain gold reserves sufficient for the volume of sales that may be necessary to peg the price of gold. And of course the Treasury is obligated to sell gold whenever the price of gold rises. Clearly any attempt to conduct discretionary monetary policy that would threaten the price of gold is ruled out.

Of course the predictable long-run value of the monetary unit depends on the predictability of the increase in the supply of gold. For the price level to maintain a constant long-run value, the long-run supply of gold would have to be perfectly elastic. Under less elastic gold supply conditions, the price level would fluctuate around a long-run deflationary trend. And if the cost of producing gold is subject to shocks such as discoveries of new ore deposits or technological improvements in the extraction process, the long-run predictability of the price level may be significantly reduced.

In any case, Anna Schwartz points out that embrace of the gold standard by the United States as a way to constrain the exercise of discretionary monetary management is not likely in the near future. Such a change in monetary arrangements would require dramatic changes that Americans are not likely to accept. It is not all certain, moreover, that prices would actually be more predictable.

Characteristics of commodity standards in general, including the gold standard, were discussed by Milton Friedman several decades ago.[5] Their shortcomings and disadvantages and advantages as monetary standards were discussed in detail by Friedman. Suffice it here to underscore, as he does, that commodity standards do have a certain automatic characteristic as well as freedom from political control provided that the commodity (e.g., gold) is the only means for changing the supply of money. Any such arrangement would require a steady accumulation of commodity stocks so as to provide for secular growth of the stock of money. As a consequence, significant resources are necessary to acquire the necessary stock of money. Any attempts to reduce the costs of such an operation will very likely involve political intervention and control—and, of course, also provides an incentive for the introduction of fiat money.

Moreover, successful international operation of such commodity standards as gold which would produce stable exchange rates requires that countries be willing to permit complete free trade in gold and submit their internal monetary and economic policies to its discipline. Clearly, this is not likely in the contemporary world economy.

It is not surprising that the U.S. Gold Commission in 1982 failed to endorse an important role for gold in American monetary arrangements. The collapse of the post–World War II Bretton Woods system along with the special role of the United States and the dollar ended operation of a gold-centered monetary system. There is no evidence that other countries are interested in the gold standard.

## FRIEDMAN'S PROPOSAL FOR REFORM

Friedman has long proposed a pure fiat currency embodied in his monetary and fiscal framework.[6] The proposal calls for a pure fiat currency issued by the government, combined with 100 percent reserve banking and the elimination of all discretionary control of the quantity of money by central bank and monetary authorities. Changes in the quantity of money would be produced entirely through the government budget. Deficits would be financed by issuing additional fiat currency, and surpluses would be used to retire the currency. The quantity of money would expand by the amount of a deficit and contract by the amount of any surplus. To provide for a secular increase in the quantity of money, the budget could include an allowance for a regular annual revenue to be derived from an addition to the supply of circulating medium.

Friedman argues that his proposal provides a national currency standard that will promote stability. At the international level, the currencies of the various countries would be connected through flexible exchange rates, freely determined in foreign-exchange markets and preferably in private dealings.

His proposal, moreover, has the additional advantage over commodity standards including gold in that it is essentially costless. It does not require the maintenance of a stock of useful goods never to be used or additional resources to the acquisition of the monetary commodity.

Friedman, of course, underscores the dangers in the explicit control of the quantity of money by government and acknowledges that the explicit creation of money to meet actual government deficits may establish a climate favorable to irresponsible government action and to inflation.[7] Moreover, he notes that the principle of a balanced budget may not be strong enough to offset these tendencies. In any case, these drawbacks in his proposal are common, he argues, with most proposals and measures arrived at via cyclical fluctuations. As he notes, such shortcomings could probably be avoided by moving to an entirely metallic currency, removing the government from the control of money, and adopting the principle of a balanced budget.

## A RULES-BASED POLICY

The issues raised by Milton Friedman decades ago remain at the center of the ongoing debate on whether monetary policy should be conducted within a rules-based system or according to the discretion of monetary authorities, including central bankers. In short, it is a debate on the nature and character of the monetary regime.

The debate itself has focused on three main reasons for constraining monetary authorities within a rules-based regime. The first reason, argued by Milton Friedman, is that monetary authorities simply lack the knowledge and information that could produce a successful discretionary policy. Long and variable time lags in the effects on the economy of monetary policy changes make discretionary fine-tuning a very risky business indeed. There is no way to be confident that discretionary fine-tuning will in fact stabilize the economy. It may very well cause greater instability. For these reasons, Milton Friedman has recommended rules for a constant rate of growth in the money supply that merit consideration.

The second reason for shunning discretionary monetary authority in favor of a rules-based one is provided by economists working within the area of rational expectations. They argue that changes in monetary policy have no effect on the course of real economic activity, including employment. People simply take into account policy changes in forming their inflationary expectations. Thus, monetary expansion leads people to expect higher inflation, which then leads them to demand higher wages, thereby leaving output and employment unchanged. Since this is the best that monetary authorities can do, so the argument goes, then they may as well operate within a rules-based policy regime, such as mandating a constant growth in the money supply, which at least minimizes the uncertainty about inflation.

Finally, the third argument is that a rules-based authority fosters the necessary credibility needed to get around the so-called problem of time inconsistency. If a monetary policy appears optimal today, but tomorrow, when the time comes for monetary authorities to act on it, it does not, then without a rules-based policy requirement, there is nothing to prevent the authorities from exercising their discretionary power and switching to what appears to be a better policy. If people believe there is nothing binding the authorities to the original policy, they may behave in ways likely to prevent the monetary authorities from achieving their original goal. Thus, the need arises for a system of rules that everyone believes the monetary authorities will abide by. It is not so much the exact nature of the rules that is important as it is the need to establish a credible commitment from monetary authorities to follow these rules.

Again, as we discussed earlier, monetary rules issues have evolved over many years. Indeed, a lineage could be established between today's proponents of monetary rules and such time-honored challengers of convention as the currency school or the "bullionists" of the nineteenth century.

Even Henry C. Simons's 1936 rules proposal was not altogether new.[8] It is clear in its underlying theoretical analysis that Simons placed great importance on the development of the quantity theory of money from John Locke to Irving Fisher. The proposal's affinity with the earlier 100 percent reserve plan is also clear.[9] Simons's first mention of monetary rules was contained in a 1934 pamphlet, where a set of rules is part of a larger program for bank reform better known today as the Chicago Plan or as economic reform in general. Among five proposals presented in a descending scale of relative importance, the proposal concerning banking and currency ranks second only to the elimination of private monopoly in all of its forms.[10]

The kinds of rules Simons referred to included, on one end of the spectrum, a constant quantity of money and, on the other end, a rule based on the stabilization of some price index. While Simons in his final position accepted a rule expressed in terms of a price index, he nevertheless felt that his earlier persuasion as to the merits of the rule of a fixed quantity of money was fundamentally correct. But the latter rule cannot be implemented, Simons argued, because we have not attained what he calls the ideal financial structure. This structure should include a sharp difference between money and private obligation in order to increase the power of the central government to create money and money substitutes.

To Simons, stabilization of a price index represented a second-best, unsatisfactory solution. On this score, Simons agrees, at least in principle, with other economists and congressional committees of his time, seeing a reason for the second-best nature of price stabilization as the difficulty presented by the definition of a particular index.[11]

Another early proponent of a monetary rule, though not in terms of a rules-oriented regime, was Carl Snyder. He concluded from his empirical analysis that as trade and production as a whole grow at a fairly fixed and definite rate, then for the maintenance of price stability, the volume of the media of exchange or bank credit must increase at the same rate.[12]

In contrast to Simons, Snyder derived his conclusion from a target-oriented, quantitative analysis. With this approach and his proposal of controlling the volume of bank credit and maintaining its increase at a fixed and predetermined rate per annum, he was surprisingly in close agreement with some of today's proponents of monetary rules.

Another contemporary and close colleague of Simons, Lloyd W. Mints, is usually associated with Simons in his ideas about the proper management of monetary policy.[13] The existing differences between Mints and Simons were more a matter of emphasis than substance. Both believed in the inherent stability of the "free" economic system; both felt that some rule would be better than none; both mentioned the desirability (and at the same time similar difficulties) concerning a constant quantity of money; and both concluded that price-level stabilization—even if difficult to implement—may be the most feasible guide to monetary policy.

Some differences do exist, however, within respective valuation of objectives or targets. For example, Mints seems to have placed greater emphasis on monetary stability per se as compared to Simons's ultimate objective of liberty. Mints also examined some questions under more technical analysis. For example, he discussed various indexes for stabilization and concluded that the wholesale price index is probably the best guide for monetary action.[14] He then expanded this discussion by also considering international aspects of the questions involved. Mints analyzed the possible effects of lags, following a suggestion by Milton Friedman, to conclude tentatively that the evidence affords no confirmation of the contention that lags in the effectiveness of changes in the stock of money might accentuate fluctuations in the level of prices.[15] Again, however, he gave no detailed description of how the guide of price-level stabilization might be translated into a simple monetary rule.

Clark Warburton and Milton Friedman also came to at least superficially similar conclusions with each other, the differences being more a matter of detail than general substance.[16] Warburton, like Friedman, arrived at his conclusions only after extensive empirical studies.[17] From these findings and inferences, Warburton derived his conclusion and resulting proposal for monetary policy: There should be a constant rate of growth in the quantity of money.

This is, at least in principle, the same conclusion reached by Friedman. However, Friedman arrived at this proposal following a different road which, at its beginning, seems to have been staked out by Simons and Mints. Friedman was an early critic of discretionary monetary policy. Through his research with Anna J. Schwartz at the National Bureau of Economic Research, he too arrived at the proposed rule that the stock of money (should) be increased at a fixed rate year in and year out.[18] His subsequent research and studies helped to underpin his initial conviction and to enlarge and specify the proposal.

A more precise delineation of the characteristics of the two proposals by Warburton and Friedman can best be achieved by comparing some of the major issues involved. The first issue is the general background of, or reason for, their respective proposals. As mentioned above, Friedman started out with a fairly strong indication for some rule and against the uncertainty and undesirable political implications of discretionary action by government authorities.[19] At the same time, however, he emphasized a possible other, more pragmatic, disadvantage of discretion—lags in response: "Long and variable lags could convert the fluctuations in the government contribution to the income stream into the equivalent of an additional random disturbance."[20] These initial premonitions about lags later became a conviction through his research on the lag in the effect of monetary policy, and the corresponding argument in favor of his proposal achieved importance. Friedman thus believed that the "contribution to economic stability" by a set of rules "is the most that we can ask from monetary policy at our present stage of knowledge," though, as he points out, "other forces would still affect the economy . . . and disturb the even tenor of our ways."[21]

Warburton, on the other hand, while not disregarding the possible effect of lags, placed less emphasis on them, and thus their existence is not as crucial to his proposal. He does view monetary policy as an overwhelmingly important factor in serious economic disturbances.

The second issue in examining the proposals of Warburton and Friedman revolves around the general framework surrounding each proposal. For Warburton, the only statutory change of major importance was the directive concerning the implementation of rule itself. While he was in favor, for example, of retirement of the Federal Reserve stock, reduction in the number of members of the Board of Governors, abolishment of regulation Q, and some of the changes with regard to reserve requirements, he emphasized how admirably the central banking machinery, with existing types of banking institutions, could serve if given proper directive by Congress.[22]

He therefore takes issue with Friedman, who regarded the rule as the most important part—but only *one* part—of desired changes in the monetary system. Among Friedman's money recommendations were the elimination of fractional-reserve banking, of the discount window, of the prohibition of interest payment on demand deposits, and of regulation Q.[23] As incisive as these changes may be, they are not indispensable. Indeed, the problem of Federal Reserve organization is not as important as putting into effect two guidelines for it to follow. The two guidelines Friedman is referring to here are (1) a constant rate of growth of the money supply and (2) competitively determined interest rates.

The third and last issue considers the more pragmatic technical aspects of the rules proposed, that is, the definition of money, seasonal adjustments, the specific rate of growth in the money supply, and the general flexibility of the rules. Both Friedman and Warburton were in favor of using an expanded version of the conventional definition of money. Whereas Friedman's proposal focused on currency held by the public, plus adjusted demand and time deposits in commercial banks, Warburton considered several other concepts as well.

Differences in emphasis seem to exist between Warburton and Friedman as to whether an allowance for seasonal variation ought to be made in the proposal. Warburton tended to favor seasonal adjustment, whereas Friedman, after initial doubts, reached the "tentative conclusion to dispense with seasonal adjustments because there is no seasonal to adjust until a decision is made on what seasonal to introduce."[24]

The remaining two questions—the actual growth rate of the money supply and its flexibility—are closely related. In their respective answers, Friedman and Warburton developed what appear to be rather marked differences. Friedman suggested growth rates between 3 and 5 percent per year and, on more theoretical grounds, a growth rate of 2 percent.[25] However, in his own words, "I have always emphasized that a steady and known rate of increase in the quantity of money is more important than the precise numerical value of the rate of increase."[26]

Warburton proposed similar growth rates with possible slight variations depending on the concept of money used. He arrived at these rates the same way Friedman did by allowing for a certain percentage decrease in secular velocity. But Warburton's emphasis seems to be more on an average range for the rate of growth in money than on its absolute constancy. When he stated that, aside from seasonal adjustments, "adjustments . . . may be needed on account of any other conditions which have been demonstrated to require variations from the calculated line of growth in the quantity of fiscal products,"[27] he created some uncertainty as to the specific content of his proposal. Compared to Friedman, who believed in a much more rigid application of the rules, Warburton seems to be closer to supporters of what might called formula flexibility.

In discussions of monetary rules, the proposal made by Edward S. Shaw is usually associated with Friedman's rigid rule, which has become known as the Friedman-Shaw proposal. A reasonable degree of similarity exists except for one major exception: Shaw's definition of money, though flexible, seems to lie more with the conventional concept.[28]

James W. Angell suggested a monetary rule that initially appears akin to Warburton's proposal, at least as far as the degree of flexibility is concerned, but Angell would apply the rule to the achievable money supply or indirectly to the commercial bank reserve base.[29] Considering the additional proposals made by him, which include more frequent use of stronger selective controls, it is obvious that Angell does not look with favor on the Warburton-Friedman proposals. On the other hand, Phillip Cagan seems to be in almost complete agreement with Warburton.[30]

Several other economists have suggested rules for formula flexibility.[31] The element that all their various proposals have in common, as compared to Warburton's rule, for example, is a built-in adjustment mechanism, leading to automatic adjustments in the rate of growth of the money supply whenever certain specified changes can be detected in the economy. These changes and the frequency with which they are to be considered represent the distinguishing elements of the proposals within this group.

Finally, no two rules are alike. The range covers the complete spectrum from almost perfect rigidity to guidelines that come very close to supporting the existing degree of discretion. This diversity within the "rules party" may help explain why there is sometimes an almost scornful reception of some of these proposals by the opposition.

## THE CRITICS

Consider now some of the major points raised by critics against monetary rules.[32] Two major points in dispute are, first, the concept of money and, second, the mechanism that links monetary and other economic variables.

The debate over the definition of money includes the issues of what is to be regarded as money now and the changing "moneyness," or liquidity of assets, because a fixed rule freezes the definition over time. The first issue is debated not only between advocates of and opponents to rules, but also within each group and among monetary economists in general. As the proposals indicate, various concepts of money have been defined, and most advocates of rules are of this opinion that a rule applied to any definition is preferable to the existing degree of discretion. Thus, it seems that the definition of money per se is not really a vital issue in the theoretical debate. The issue of the flexibility over time of the concept of money may be more important, but it is obviously also a matter of the degree of specific flexibility built into the rule. No proposal is regarded "as the be-all and end-all of monetary policy for all time."[33]

The link between the stock of money and reserve is discussed in the velocity of money and more specifically, in the variability or stability of velocity. Proponents of rules believe in a relatively stable and predictable velocity, whereas opponents tend to regard velocity as subject to erratic variations. Without analyzing all the details and individual differences, suffice it to say that these differences are no longer as sharp as they were formerly.

A similar statement could be made about time lags, where the concern centers on three elements: (1) definition or measurement of lags, (2) their length or distribution, and (3) their variability. Typically, long and variable lags are associated with proponents of rules, whereas short lags are associated with opponents to rules. Friedman is the only one among the proponents who makes explicit allowance for the variability of lags. Also, while a few proponents seem to share the belief in at least the possibility of relatively long lags, any dividing line, if it is be to drawn, does not follow the established rules-versus-discretion discussion. The laziness appears to be mainly a consequence of the lack of definitude in the theoretical issues.

Although the control of the stock of money under the present system is subject to adequate forecasting by the Federal Reserve, the issue of effective control is not restricted to monetary rules. After the money supply is accepted as an indicator or subtarget, any rational monetary policy implies effective control of the money supply as a prerequisite. Whether the present Federal Reserve System complies with the prerequisite is therefore a broader, much more basic question of monetary policy.

The essence of the differences between critics and proponents of monetary rules can be cast as another question: can the target(s) be achieved more effectively and precisely by rules or by discretion? Two specific arguments can be usefully noted. The first is the often heard critique that monetary rules are characterized by the implicit precept: Ignore fiscal policy. The second is that the obstacle to rules is that several ends are in complex and unstable rivalry or conflict with each other.

The first argument appears overdrawn. Proponents of rules simply do not ignore fiscal policy. Whereas quite a few supporters rely more heavily on monetary policy, this cannot be interpreted as a subscription that only money matters. Indeed, the objective is to procreate economic stability even if, as some critics argue, money does not matter.

The second argument implies the hypothesis that conflicting objections can be served more effectively by a monetary authority that is to use its best judgment each time that a decision of some sort is called for as to the relative weight to be given to the objectives. Aside from the question of whether this kind and degree of discretion is compatible with the economic and political system, the intuitive nature of the argument hinges on another, more institutioned, issue—the relative fallibility or infallibility of the monetary authority.[34]

## NOTES

1.   "Monetary Policy Mysteries," *The Economist* 7985, September 28, 1996, p. 96.

2.   Ibid., p. 96.

3.   Ibid., p. 96.

4.   *Report to the Congress of the Commission on the Role of Gold in the Domestic and International Monetary System*, Vols. 1 and 2. (Washington, D.C.: The Secretary of the Treasury, March 1982). See also Anna J. Schwartz, "Introduction," in *A Retrospective on the Classical Gold Standard, 1821–1931*, ed. Michael D. Bordo and Anna J. Schwartz (Chicago: University of Chicago Press, 1984), pp. 1–20.

5.   Milton Friedman, "Commodity-Reserve Currency," *Journal of Political Economy* 59 (June 1951) pp. 203–32. Reprinted in Milton Friedman, ed., *Essays in Positive Economics* (Chicago: University of Chicago Press, 1953), pp. 204–50.

6.   Milton Friedman, "A Monetary and Fiscal Framework for Economic Stability," in *Essays in Positive Economics,* ed. Milton Friedman (Chicago: University of Chicago Press, 1953), pp. 133–56.

7.   Ibid., p. 156.

8.   Henry C. Simons, "Rules versus Authorities in Monetary Policy," *Journal of Political Economy* 4 (February 1936), pp. 1–30.

9.   For a discussion of this and similar plans, see Albert G. Hart, "The Chicago Plan for Banking Reform," *Review of Economic Studies* 2 (1935), pp. 104–16.

10.   Henry C. Simons, "A Positive Program for Laissez-Faire: Some Proposals for a Liberal Economic Policy," in *Public Policy Pamphlet*, No. 15, ed. H. D. Gideonse (Chicago: University of Chicago Press, 1934).

11.   See Irving Fisher, *Stabilizing the Dollar* (New York: Macmillan, 1920); U.S. Congress, House Committee on Banking and Currency, *Stabilization Hearings* before Committee on Banking and Currency, Stabilization Hearings, House of Representatives on H.R. 11806, 7th Cong., 1st sess., 1928; U.S. Congress, Senate Committee on Banking and Currency, *Restoring and Maintaining the Average Purchasing Power of the Dollar*, Hearings before Committee on Banking and Currency, Senate, on H.R. 11499 and S. 4429, 72d Cong., 1st sess., 1932.

12.   Carl Snyder, "The Problem of Monetary and Economic Stability," *Quarterly Journal of Economics* 49 (February 1935), p. 198.

13. See Lloyd W. Mints, *Monetary Policy for a Competitive Society* (New York: McGraw-Hill, 1950), pp. 115–73; Mints, "Monetary Policy and Stabilization," *American Economic Review Papers and Proceedings* 41 (May 1951), pp. 188–93.

14. Mints, *Monetary Policy for a Competitive Society*, p. 136.

15. Ibid., p. 142.

16. For a comparative summary of Warburton's and Friedman's proposals, see Richard T. Selden, "Stable Monetary Growth," in U.S. Congress, House, Committee on Banking and Currency, *Compendium on Monetary Policy Guidelines and Federal Reserve Structure*, Pursuant to H.R. 11, Subcommittee on Domestic Finance of the Committee on Banking and Currency, House of Representatives, 90th Cong., 2d sess., 1968 (hereinafter referred to as *Compendium*), pp. 324–31.

17. See Clark Warburton, "The Volume of Money and Price Lead Between the World Wars," *Journal of Political Economy* 53, (1945), pp. 150–63; Warburton, "Rules and Implements of Monetary Policy," *Journal of Finance* 8 (March 1953), pp. 1–21.

18. Milton Friedman and Anna J. Schwartz, *A Monetary History of the United States* (Princeton: Princeton University Press, 1963).

19. Friedman, "Monetary and Fiscal Framework," p. 263.

20. Ibid., p. 254.

21. Milton Friedman, "The Role of Monetary Policy," *American Economic Review* 58 (March 1968), p. 17.

22. Warburton, "Rules and Implements of Monetary Policy," pp. 1–21.

23. Milton Friedman, *A Program for Monetary Stability*, The Millar Lectures, No. 3 (New York: Fordham University Press, 1968), pp. 100–102.

24. Ibid., p. 92.

25. Milton Friedman, *The Optimal Quantity of Money and Other Essays* (Chicago: Aldine, 1969), pp. 45–48.

26. Ibid., p. 48.

27. Warburton, "Rules and Implements of Monetary Policy," p. 7; as examples of such conditions, Warburton mentions change in short-run velocity and changes in the rate of growth of population and productivity.

28. Edward S. Shaw, "Monetary Stability in a Growing Economy," in *The Allocation of Economic Resources: Essays in Honor of B. F. Haley*, ed. Edward S. Shaw (Stanford: Stanford University Press, 1959), pp. 218–35.

29. James W. Angell, "Appropriate Monetary Policy and Operations in the United States Today," *Review of Economics and Statistics* 42 (August 1960), pp. 247–52.

30. Phillip Cagan, Statement, in *Compendium*, p. 106.

31. Martin Bronfenbrenner, "Monetary Rules: A New Look," *Journal of Law and Economics* 8 (October 1965), pp. 173–94.

32.   See, for instance, Lyle E. Gramley, "Guidelines for Monetary Policy: The Case against Simple Rules," in *Readings in Money, National Income, and Stabilization Policy,* revised, ed. W. L. Smith and R. L. Teigan ( Homewood, IL: Irwin, 1970), pp. 488–93.

33.   Friedman, *Program for Monetary Stability*, p. 98.

34.   See, for instance, Charles R. Whittlesey, "Rules, Discretion, and Central Bankers," in *Essays in Money and Banking in Honour of Richard S. Sayers*, ed. C. R. Whittlesey and J. S. Wilson (London: Oxford University Press, 1968), pp. 252–65.

# 4

## The Garrison or Warfare State

### THE LEGACY

The role that governments now play in economic affairs seems to be changing. The end of the Cold War and a bipolar ideological world has brought with it significant worldwide changes. Along with these changes, the focus of government programs need no longer be support for a "garrison or warfare state" and the large military-industrial complex that sustained it.

New forms of government intervention may well come into force. New forms of regulation are to be expected. Whether a free-market ideology will replace the mercantilism of the garrison state remains to be seen. The idea that an active government can do better than the market in achieving its goals of strengthening and improving the long-term prospects of the economy is not new. In many respects, this view is a legacy of the 1930s and the Keynesian Revolution and its research agenda.

The rapid changes in the world's social, economic, and political affairs that began during the late 1920s and the 1930s Great Depression provided the atmosphere favorable to the Keynesian research agenda. In particular, the change in the role of the state since that time is generally associated with the Keynesian Revolution. The ideas associated with the Keynesian research agenda included the view that the economy was not self-equilibrating and self-adjusting. Only the state was capable of raising and controlling aggregate expenditure which would enable maximum employment of a country's resources, including labor. No one else had the power to do so.

World War II underscored and increased the role of the state in mobilizing and controlling the resources of the nation. After the war, the United States found itself deeply engaged in reconstruction and the Cold War. In the following years, the country was intensely preoccupied with the Cold War. Unlike the case in the years following World War I, America did not relinquish control of resources to the private sector. The armaments made necessary by the Cold War confrontation on a worldwide scale had evolved to a scientific and technological level beyond the reach of the market sector and private consumer demand. The net result was that the American government and state became the direct or indirect employer of the bulk of the country's scientific and technological resources. For all practical purposes, the Cold War served to increase government intervention and regulation in the country's economic, political, and social affairs.

By not challenging the country's basic ideological foundation, the Keynesian Revolution managed to change American policy prescription to encourage and strengthen government intervention. Few if any Keynesians directly challenged the conception at the center of neo-classical economics and the free competitive market economy of individual self-seekers. They were always supportive of the operation of a competitive, market-directed economic system. They focused instead on managing aggregate expenditures by encouraging or discouraging private investment through central bank manipulation of the money supply and interest rates and by the judicious budgeting of surplus/deficit at the source of public spending. The new activity for the state provided by Keynesian doctrines served the government well in mobilizing and controlling resources during the Great Depression, World War II, and the years of the Cold War.

Thus, the Keynesian apparatus provided the necessary theoretical and policy apparatus for the active participation by government in the country's economy. In crisis after crisis, government is driven by the country's needs and expectations to undertake more and more central and complex responsibilities. There is no other instrument or agency to do what needs to be done, in the view of Keynesians and the supporters of their research agenda, or in the very broad view, of their "paradigm." The Great Depression put into place a redesigned government. It became the task of the government through monetary and fiscal manipulations, through transfer payments, and through changes in the rules of the market game, to offset instabilities, insecurities, and inequities of the free-enterprise market economy. This neoclassical synthesis was as much political economy as it was economic analysis.

The declining attractiveness of the Keynesian research agenda and the end of the Cold War decades of ideological confrontation between political entities underscores that change is in the offing.

In retrospect, the neoclassical synthesis consisting of Keynesian macroeconomics and neoclassical microeconomics dominated economic policy during the Cold War. It served to complement President Harry S. Truman's doctrine (the Truman Doctrine) for the containment of communism. In fact, the Truman Doctrine in the 1950s and 1960s aimed at more than containment of communism. Containment and pressure on the communist bloc would ultimately bring about a breakdown of that system and thus eliminate it as a threat to the United States and the West. The Western democracies, on the other hand, would continue to prosper, thanks to their embrace of the neoclassical synthesis. In sum, the neoclassical synthesis defined the policy mix that would allow Western capitalism not only to survive, but to win the Cold War.

## MILITARY-INDUSTRIAL COMPLEX

The Cold War engulfed the United States and its allies in the post–World War II years. On the sweeping tides of tension rode the evil trinity of fear, distrust, and suspicion, and it rode so hard and so well that soon no man could tell where truth ended and propaganda began. Both in the United States and in the Soviet Union, there developed a hardening of official attitudes, a growth of distrust and suspicion that made candid talk impossible, and a hunt for "solutions" in the only way it seemed they could be found, in even greater reliance on massive armaments, on weapons of "defense" to guard against the intangible but imminent aggression. This was indeed a new road for the United States to travel. It was the road to a garrison or warfare state. Both the military who would handle the weapons of total destruction under the banner of total safety and the industrial sector that would produce those weapons were ready and willing to undertake the mission. This indeed is the military-industrial complex that President Dwight D. Eisenhower warned against in the closing years of his administration.

In fact, no break with the traditions of America's past has been so complete, so drastic, as the one that has resulted in the growth of the Cold War military-industrial complex. President Eisenhower pictured it as a colossus that had come to dominate vast areas of American life. He had fought a long-continued and not always noted battle with this colossus. Though it was undeclared and unproclaimed, Eisenhower waged a guerrilla war with the multibillion dollar might of the military-industrial complex.

There are many examples of Eisenhower's efforts throughout two terms to hold down the more extravagant demands of the military services and to keep the defense budget within bounds. On more than one occasion, he gave vent to testy expressions of concern. He often stressed that material survival depended upon solvency with security. During his battle with Congress over reorganization, he criticized overindulgence in sentimental attachments to outmoded military equipment and doctrines. When asked in 1959 whether he would spend more for national defense, he replied that he would not. He underscored that unless military spending was restricted, the United States would become "a garrison state," with all its energies concentrated on military production.

In more than one instance, Eisenhower's military acumen and civilian leadership were both at stake. A case in point is the so-called missile-gap controversy, which he promptly denounced as a fraud. Repeatedly he denied the existence of any gap; he repudiated the suggestion that his administration, in its desire to balance the budget, had left the United States virtually defenseless.

The issue of the missile gap was promoted by the air force, evidently with the purpose of getting more millions and more bombers. The impact on public consciousness was significant, and feelings of alarm spread throughout the country. The charge that the Eisenhower administration, in its concern for budgetary discipline, had let down American defenses became one of the key issues of the 1960 presidential campaign, and President Kennedy, having used the missile-gap controversy for all the political mileage that was in it, came to office irrevocably pledged, irrevocably committed, to boosting military spending to new heights.

Very soon after the Kennedy administration was firmly in place the truth came out; there never had been a missile gap. Indeed, if there had been one, it was in America's favor.

Such experiences formed the background for Eisenhower's decision to warn against the threat to democracy posed by the growth of the military-industrial complex. He concluded that even with his prestige as America's foremost general and president, he found it almost impossible to deal with the political, bureaucratic, and propagandistic pressures generated by the military-industrial complex. He recognized that his successor would be civilian, without his military expertise and reputation to back up his judgment when this judgment conflicted with the desires of the military-industrial complex. Certainly Eisenhower is to be applauded for his warning, which even today should not be taken lightly.

Eisenhower's views are certainly consistent with those of the Founding Fathers. The great leaders of the day were all genuinely concerned with the issues Eisenhower addressed. They shared concern lest the military arrogate to itself the kind of power that ultimately might lead it to dominate the state.

As a matter of fact, various other statesmen, politicians, and responsible observers had underscored the necessity of separating the military from the industrial component of the complex. Thus, Senator William J. Fulbright (D., Ark.), early in the Cold War, attempted to strip the military half from the industrial half of this mighty complex. To many people with vested interests in the complex, Fulbright posed a real threat if his advice to limit the military to providing only technical advice and refraining from political activity was to be heeded. If the military was to be curbed, the whole structure that fed those multiple billions of dollars into the treasury of big industry—and watered the economy of the entire country—might begin to collapse.

The charge that Senator Fulbright was attempting to "muzzle" the military clouded the real issue that he was trying to prevent the kind of military dominance of public policy that, in Japan, had led to Tojo and in Germany, to Hitler. He noted that military attempts to educate the public on the nature of the communist threat tended to garb itself in the radicalism of the right. It offered the simple solution, easily understood: scourging of the devils within the body politic or, in the extreme, lashing out at the economy.

The American people, Fulbright argued, had little need to be alerted to the menace of communism and the Cold War. On the contrary, he noted, the need was for an understanding of the true nature of the threat, and the direction of the public's present and foreseeable awareness of the fact of the threat toward support of the president's own program for survival in a nuclear age. In his view, there were no reasons to believe that military personnel generally could contribute to this need beyond their specific technical competence to explain their own role. Rather, he argued, there were many reasons and some evidence for believing that an effort by the military, beyond this limitation, involved considerable danger.

Senator Fulbright's warning regarding military involvement in educating the public on the menace of communism and the Cold War and its relation to the country's industrial sector provoked a hurricane of controversy that he never expected. In high-minded concern, he evidently had no conception that he was on to a very sensitive issue in the military-industrial complex. The idea of stripping the military frontmen, who could command public respect for its policies as the industrial heads of the other half of the complex could not, was indeed a serious challenge to the complex. Reaction to Fulbright's comments was testament in itself to a startling fact—the extent to which it was well financed and promoted.

Today we recall with amazement the so-called experts of the 1950s and 1960s in estimating for the American people the probable magnitude of the country's losses in a nuclear war. We had been constantly assured by spokesmen like Henry A. Kissinger that a nuclear war was possible, or by Herman Kahn, the longtime associate of Rand, that nuclear war, however horrible, was so "bearable" that American society, in ten years, could be restored virtually to its prewar state.

What are we to make of these views of nuclear war expressed by these widely accepted realists and experts of those years? Surely, when one weighs the prospects of war, one should ponder the worst, not the best, that may happen, and if one doesn't, one can hardly lay claim to the title of hardheaded realist. For one thing history teaches us is that in war nothing ever happens quite the way the optimistic warriors, who think they have everything planned so nicely, have convinced themselves it will.

In marked contrast to the 1950s and 1960s, we now have in the mid and late 1990s former military leaders around the world calling for the elimination of nuclear weapons. This is, indeed, a stunning reversal for many of these people. For decades, they stood ready to launch a nuclear war, the consequences be damned. Now they are saying that these weapons are obscene and their effects unspeakable. All indicate their fear that the chance to speed nuclear disarmament presented by the Cold War's end is fast slipping away. We can well agree that we can indeed do better than condone a world in which nuclear weapons are accepted as commonplace.

Other analysts take the generals to task for promoting the notion that destroying America's nuclear arsenal will solve the country's principal foreign policy challenges. Their critics argue that the generals' idea is worse than a distraction; it is a dangerous delusion.[1]

According to their critics, America's goal should be to continue to reduce and stabilize the American and Russian nuclear arsenals. The goal should be to continue these efforts and concentrate on better ways of stopping the flow of nuclear technology and materials to outlaw states. Indeed, to call for stabilization of America's nuclear arsenal assumes that the declared nuclear powers will agree not only to destroy their weapons, but to do so in concert. Critics note that the day that all great powers are prepared to do this together is the day the history of international relations as we have known it for three and a half centuries will have ended.[2]

While the idealism of the generals and others is to be applauded, their idea should be rejected. The abolition of nuclear weapons is simply impractical. You cannot, according to their critics, disinvent an idea. The technology to build nuclear weapons is widespread, and eliminating them from America's arsenal will not keep them from appearing elsewhere.

Certainly, nuclear weapons are expensive and dangerous. Eliminating them is no less so. A case in point is the problem caused by the dismantling of American and Russian nuclear weapons and of getting rid of thousands of plutonium pits from the warheads that are rapidly accumulating in each country. In 1996–1997, America will need to dispose of more than fifty tons of excess plutonium. Russia has an even greater stockpile. Until these basketball-sized nuclear cores are somehow neutralized, they pose a double threat. Either nation could reverse the course of disarmament and stick the warhead plutonium right back into new weapons, or thieves, especially in economically distressed Russia, might steal some pits for use in bombs by terrorists or renegade nations.

## COLD WAR BLUEPRINTS FOR A POST–COLD WAR WORLD?

Exactly what are the national interests of the United States in the post–Cold War era, and how can they best be advanced? Consider, for instance, the Clinton administration's push toward an eastward expansion of NATO by the end of the decade. This push apparently is underway without adequate discussion with the American people and Congress. To be sure, the issue is remote and abstract to many Americans. Nevertheless, NATO expansion provides a topic well worth a thorough

American discussion. The expansion would involve a crucial political and military realignment of Europe.

Among other things, NATO expansion would commit the United States to the defense of former Warsaw Pact countries as well as to a very costly modernization of their military forces. At the same time, such a step would almost surely strengthen Russian nationalists and communists still traumatized by the invasion of Germany and its allies in two world wars.

The need for such an expansion needs to be clearly demonstrated and its potential consequences more carefully considered. Simply dressing up its plans with rhetoric about consolidating democracy, free markets, and the usual trappings is inadequate. Why, for instance, should a Cold War alliance now be in a better position to secure such aims than the European Union. Surely Cold War blueprints are a poor way to plan and build a future Europe.

The nonsense that passes for analysis by various vested interests surely leaves something to be desired. Does Russia really present a threat to world peace? With a shattered, impoverished military and faltering economy, the country presents no military threat to its neighbors now, nor indeed for many years to come. NATO expansion is very likely, if anything, to provoke Russia toward precisely the kind of rearmament the West fears. It is also the very thing that Russia least needs as it struggles to rid itself of decades of communism. The central issue in the post–Cold War period surely is the consolidation of reform and democracy in Russia.

If NATO expansion is indeed to be a cornerstone of America's post–Cold War policy, it lacks compelling strategic vision. The Clinton administration's second-term foreign policy team has a strong potential for the politicization of foreign policy. If that happens, the Clinton administration may well lose public and congressional confidence. Fortunately, there is still time for the public and Congress to consider the implications of NATO expansion and to slow the stampede to move the alliance's boundaries closer to Russia. There is still hope, since none of this can happen without the approval of two-thirds of the United States Senate as well as the approval of the parliaments of the alliance's fifteen European members.

The Russians, for their part, are attempting to contain the potentially destructive domestic consequences of NATO expansion. Whatever the ultimate consequences of planning with Cold War blueprints by the foreign policy experts may be, the American public will realize soon enough that the policy lacks strategic sense. The case is yet to be made why a Cold War military alliance is the best way to consolidate democracy and free markets in a post–Cold War Europe. The exercise simply underscores the confusion about what the national interests of the United States are in the post–Cold War period.

Few will doubt that America has changed in the years since World War II. It has been changed by the Cold War years and the warfare or garrison state. Some critics argue that the United States had become imperialistic in the ideological sense. They argue that America had embraced the Marxist-Leninist concept of inevitable battle to the death between incompatible systems. The goal of the warfare state in America was not, according to these critics, the preservation of peace and law and order in the world, but the extension of the capitalistic system throughout the world at the expense of the communist system. Transformation to a post–Cold War world will not be easy even for the United States, the victor. It will be particularly difficult if we insist on using Cold War blueprints to plan the transformation.

The world is simply too vast, too complex, to be ruled or contained by any one people or system. No power yet has ever proved equal to the task; almost certainly no power ever will. Yet this is the course upheld by those who argue that the United States is the only superpower and so it alone must lead and commit whatever resources are necessary to do so. This is a policy of folly, and we can only end in impoverishing and ruining America.

We have ample examples from history of some of the great empires of Europe that have come and gone, beginning with ancient Egypt and Rome, and in more recent years, Spain, the dominant power for some two hundred years.[3] Spain was followed by the Netherlands, which became the financial center of Europe and the leading sea power. The Netherlands was followed by England, which dominated the last century and created the greatest empire ever known. The ideal of a post–Cold War world dominated by the United States is meaningless, since resources move effortlessly across national frontiers and in the process lose their national identities.

The United States committed its resources for decades to a holy crusade to contain communism, to beat it back into its Russian lair, and there to slowly strangle it. The country relied for success in this battle almost wholly on two resources—arms and money—that are in the final analysis limited, not infinite. For years, the country had waged a war of ideological imperialism not in ideological terms, by which it was finally won, but in strictly military terms, by which it could never have been won. America has exported its money and military hardware. It has not adequately exported its ideals. All too often in the Cold War decades, American definition of the "free world" has included decadent dynasties and ruthless dictators only because of their assurance that their hearts are anticommunist.

Some observers argue that not until the Kennedy administration took office did the United States begin to recognize that the basic Cold War struggle involved the minds and lives of men and women, not the weight of competing megatons. Kennedy's Peace Corps and his Alliance for Progress in South America expressed, in the view of these observers, American idealism at its best and represented the kind of effort to improve the lives of people, to effect change by peaceful means, that can win converts and offer the poverty-stricken, disease-ridden peoples of the world an alternative to communism. These observers also underscore that such programs had to wait until 1961 to be born, and it is significant that even then, the same Congress that voted unquestioning billions for military arms and military foreign aid growled about such impractical idealism, and pinched pennies.

The military fixations of the warfare state during the Cold War had led many Americans to dismiss the validity and power of ideas and ideals. Yet, it is idealism, even if mistaken idealism, that has been the dynamo of revolutions and the course of the overthrow of the most powerful of regimes and the most ruthless of dictators. No amount of money and no quantity of military hardware could have insured victory over communism unless they were backed by the faith of people. To this end, it was and is essential to make democracy real and the vehicle of social, political, and economic change. The creeping authoritarianism of the warfare state ill served such ideals.

It is important that the United States draw the correct conclusions from its experiences with the warfare state for the now post–Cold War period. Certainly one conclusion is that what is needed is a restoration of sanity to the American domestic scene and a firmer commitment to the basic principles of America's democracy. Labels hastily pinned on by arts of propaganda—a well-known device of the warfare state—can no longer substitute for debate and thought.

It is important to promote the freewheeling and vigorous debate that is the lifeblood of democracy. This debate should certainly include American participation in hazardous foreign adventures where the country has no vital interests and where as a matter of practical common sense, America simply does not belong. Otherwise, America will be condemned to wear a military scowl and to follow courses that are contrary to its strategic interests. Tinkering with the affairs of the world should be done, if at all, with great caution and a strong sense of humility. This is important if the country is to avoid being dragged helplessly by the architects of such tinkering from brink to brink and on to disaster from which there may be no return.

Attempts to work from Cold War blueprints surely make little sense in the contemporary world. For instance, some observers now focus on culture as an organizing principle of foreign policy to replace ideology. Accordingly, in the future the fundamental source of conflict in the post–Cold War world will not be primarily ideological or economic. The source of conflict will be cultural. Samuel Huntington claims that future conflicts and wars would occur between nations and groups of different civilizations (e.g., Western, Confucian, Japanese, Islamic, Hindu, Orthodox, Latin American, African, and Buddhist). Their disputes would, in the future, dominate global politics. In effect, global politics will be reconfigured along cultural lines.[4]

Increasingly, analysts are examining the influence of cultural values and institutions in the post–Cold War world. Some writers focus on culture and the economy. Here the idea is that cultural values and norms equip people and their countries either well or poorly for economic success. Max Weber's work on the Protestant work ethic is an example. The Protestant areas of Germany and Switzerland, he argued, are more developed for that reason than the Catholic areas.

Another group of analysts considers the link between cultural factors and political systems. In their view, democracy is not something that can be put on like a coat; it is part of a country's social fabric and takes many years to develop.

A third group of scholars focuses on the way in which cultural factors influence decision making. One consequence of such differences is that people from different countries see the same issue in different ways owing to their differing cultural backgrounds. Such differences may well lead to misperception in international relations. Examples are readily at hand, ranging from trade disputes to war.

It is not surprising that these various views of cultural influences have provoked arguments. The difficulty is to define culture. It is a slippery and perhaps too broad concept for most people. They tend to prefer a narrower identity, such as an ethnic group or country. To be sure, ethnic or national identity can coexist with wider cultural identification. Even here, however, a narrower loyalty can blunt the wider one because national characteristics are often considered unique or special (e.g., English exceptionalism).

Much has been said of Islam, in whose case it is argued that culture dominates over national identification. Nevertheless, even here nationhood remains strong (e.g., Egyptian, Iraqi, and Iranian Islamic values may or may not be the antithesis of modernizing Western values). Islam is also a monotheistic religion, which encourages rationalism and science.

A conclusion that one can easily reach is that cultures are so complicated that they can seldom be used to explain behavior accurately. The same culture can produce wholly different effects at different times. Moreover, cultures seldom operate in isolation. All sorts of other factors come to influence known behavior at the same time. The best that can be done is to gauge roughly the importance of culture in any given situation.

Important as cultural factors may well be for both individuals and countries, it is unlikely that such factors will overwhelm the importance of government or economic and political factors. Culture does not appear to play the same all-embracing role that ideology played during the Cold War. Ethnic and religious strife aside, unique cultures may well be declining, owing to rapid globalization of trade and tastes.[5] To be sure, there will always be a good deal of tailoring of products and services to accommodate local tastes and preferences so as to avoid a cultural backlash. The need for such cultural sensitivity is underscored when a globalization is viewed as Americanization.

Short of the use of force, which is highly unlikely, Russia will not get its empire back. The military is certainly in no position to undertake any such project in the near future. Many of the countries of Eastern and Central Europe are now becoming, albeit slowly, working market economies, if not complete democracies in the Jeffersonian sense. Moreover, it is now becoming clear just how poorly the communist economies have performed.

Analysts have produced some rough estimates of how much time the former communist-socialist countries will need just to catch up to their

European neighbors. In 1937, Czechoslovakia was more prosperous than Spain or Greece and nearly on a level with Austria, Italy, and Ireland. After almost two generations under communist-socialist rule, Czechoslovakia, though the most prosperous of the East–Central European countries, was now poorer than the poorest Western European country. Its standard of living was barely a third of neighboring Austria's. Every other country in East–Central Europe similarly lost ground. The studies suggest that it will very likely take these countries more than two decades even to approach Western standards of living. In effect, two generations of failed economies have cost them at least a generation of lost income.

To be sure, these estimates are rough, but they do suggest that Russia, which started farther behind and spent three generations under a similar socioeconomic-political system, will be many years working itself out of the depths into which it was plunged in 1917.

It will indeed take considerable time for these countries to rid themselves of the economic, political, and psychological drag of their past immersion in Marxism. The attractiveness of Marxist socialist-communist ideology was based on the belief that it could and would create a society free of want. In many respects, it was the by-product of the Industrial Revolution and capitalism as it was practiced at that time. In fact, Karl Marx focused on the inequities that the Industrial Revolution cast up. Communism proclaimed the building of God's kingdom on earth and happiness to humankind. It simply could not deliver on its promises. Instead, it promoted a tightly controlled economic and political system run by the Communist Party. No withering away of the state and no emancipation of the proletariat occurred.

## NOTES

1. See Richard N. Haas, "It's Dangerous to Disarm: The U.S. Needs Its Nuclear Arsenal," *New York Times*, Wednesday, December 11, 1996, p. A21.

2. Ibid.

3. For instance, see Paul Kennedy, *The Rise and Fall of Great Powers* (New York: Random House, 1988).

4. "Cultural Explanations," *The Economist* 341, no. 7991, November 9, 1996, pp. 23–26. See also the books and other sources mentioned in the article, especially the studies by Samuel Huntington.

5. See George Macesich, *Transformation and Emerging Markets* (Westport, CT: Praeger, 1996).

# 5

## Problems in the Emerging Economies

### EUROPE

Many emerging countries have implemented impressive reforms.[1] However, economics and, in some instances, performance have not yet met expectations. The reforms are the consequence of two developments. One is the fall of communism. The other is the ability and willingness of businesses to internationalize their activities to maximize profits and minimize costs.

These developments were not received with enthusiasm by everyone. In Europe the dread, particularly on the left, is that Europe will become like the United States, a society it regards as ruthless and uncaring. The response to globalization, according to this view, should not be simply the importation of the American model. And of course, politicians from Bonn to Athens, anxious about staying competitive in an increasingly globalized economy, are trying to figure out how to trim a generous system of benefits, long holidays and maternity leaves, free medical care, and other state-paid perks without upsetting the societies that have grown up on them.

In the contest for public support, even literal Marxists such as Italy's Communist Refounding Party are seeking a role.[2] The importance of this party for Italy is the influence it holds in the country's national policies. Although not part of Italy's ruling center-left coalition, the Communist Refounding won 8.6 percent of the vote in April 1996, and it holds the key to successful passage of reform. It provides the votes the coalition needs to pass its program in the lower house of Parliament, and indeed to continue to govern.

Led by Fausto Bertinotti, and consisting of a mix of workers, intellectuals, environmentalists, and feminists, the party is not very different from what it was in the late 1980s. To be sure, the Cold War is over and Moscow is no longer a point of reference. For its members the class struggle is still on, capitalists are still the enemy, and Pope John Paul II gets a standing ovation, but only for his critique of the tyranny of market economies.

According to Mr. Bertinotti, communism still represents a search for equality. Its fall in Eastern Europe in no way diminishes this search for equality by the party. The party's task, among others, is to protect the social achievements of the last fifty years, a task it shares with all others who protest the cutbacks in social spending.

The net effect is that other people consider the party's position as nothing less than the imposition of communist ideology on the Italian government and the middle class, which is the productive force in the country. Their criticism shares the skepticism in other parts of Europe, Germany in particular, about Italy's ability to keep its promises of fiscal responsibility.

Habits and institutions cannot be transformed overnight. A look at Eastern Europe suggests the depth of ongoing problems. On the positive side, Russia, for instance, plans to surrender its large stakes in big companies to special trusteeships by 1997, bypassing a law that delays sell-offs for several years. Under a presidential decree that signals a victory for reformers, the Russian government will transfer its controlling stakes to trustees, who will oversee management before the companies are sold off. In 1996, Russia, with its privatization plan 70 percent complete, still had big holdings in about 3,000 companies. On the minus side, Russia continued in 1996 in a deep economic crisis: Gross Domestic Product had been falling since 1991. Many workers had gone unpaid for months.

In the rest of Eastern Europe, the results are also mixed. Some countries are registering positive economic and political results. Others are basket cases. Many of the countries have considerable industrial capacity that is idle, as well as many unemployed workers. To be sure, a good part of the industrial capital is obsolete. The Czech Republic, which is the richest of the former communist countries, had a Gross Domestic

Product per capita of about $8,000 in 1996. This is about one half the average in the European Union and one-third of that in the United States.

On a more positive note, many of the Eastern European countries have a well-educated labor force. Their primary and secondary school systems are about as good as those in the leading industrial countries. Certainly their schools are superior to those of many other emerging economies. A shrinking labor force in the Eastern European countries, together with a rapidly increasing number of pensioners, will certainly pose serious problems in these countries. A case in point is Hungary, where there is one pensioner for every five people of working age.

Most observers agree that emerging countries should focus on promoting freer trade and small government and encouraging saving and investment. To judge from available evidence, the Eastern European countries have much work ahead of them if they are to improve their performance.[3]

For example, in a number of emerging countries with rapid economic growth, public spending averaged 15 percent of Gross Domestic Product in 1996; in the Eastern European countries, the figure was around 50 percent. A good part of the difference can be attributed to pensions and other welfare payments. Another striking difference is the saving rates, which averaged 30 percent of the Gross Domestic Product in the rapidly growing countries compared to 17 percent in Hungary and 21 percent in the Czech Republic. High domestic savings is required to pay for the capital acquisition needed for growth, even though some investment can be financed by foreign sources. If current policies continue, it will take the Eastern European countries years to match the performance of the leading emerging countries.

The lessons that these studies suggest are that Eastern European countries would do well to look for inspiration in the rapidly growing emerging countries rather than copying the social welfare schemes of the European Union countries. Accordingly, they should reduce existing welfare costs and raise domestic savings. Such policies may well yield results that thus far have eluded Eastern Europe.

The societies in East and Central Europe are in transition, though it is not clear that this transition is to the kind of democracy favored by many people in the West. This underscores what should be clear by now: although societies do change, it is a myth to think that they can be turned upside down—at least peacefully. The continuities between conditions before and after the removal of Marxist communism in the region are striking.

It is not surprising that the economic crises characteristic of these countries enforce the leadership's desire to adopt a policy of protectionism rather than of free trade. To these ends, secure frontiers are necessary to protect the outflow of existing resources and the inflow of immigrants, refugees, and other problems.

Secure frontiers require a strong state to enforce them. With the wobbly nature of many of these states and their governments' inability to enforce the frontiers, the leadership typically turns to ethnic inclusion and exclusion. As a result, people identify each other by ethnicity rather than citizenship. One consequence of the breakdown of state authority and police power is that those minority citizens without a strong and nearby patron state are at risk.

Regimes in these former socialist states were ideologically future oriented; the current leadership attempts to distance itself by adopting and cultivating a distant and mystic past. This is to serve in place of an absent and credible program of reconstruction and political and social integration. The practices of recasting old symbols, including flags, currency, and other trappings from a golden era, are standard. Unfortunately, for a number of these socialist successor states, this involves celebrating a fascist and/or equally odious past (e.g., in Croatia and Slovakia).

The previous regimes in these countries managed to destroy whatever institutions of autonomous collective action existed before the communists came to power. Various church organizations managed to survive, if not prosper, under the communists. As a result, churches tend to provide some modicum of guidance and focus in an otherwise associational wasteland. It is little wonder that ethnicity and nationalism now serve as guidance for collective action. In effect, they have displaced the state-dependent organizations and the authoritarian mobilization of collective action.

The ethnification of politics and intolerance toward other groups may be driven by the rational calculation that no fair and stable solutions of ethnic conflict are possible, whether agreed upon by groups in question or imposed from the outside. This indeterminacy is reinforced by the urgency with which the various ethnic groups now view the distribution of territory, sovereignty, and other resources. They may consider it appropriate to lay claim to what they consider rightfully theirs.

As to why there is no fair and impartial way to settle ethnic conflict, observers note that given the mixed population in many areas in question, as in Europe, it is impossible to draw territorial boundaries around homogenous populations. Moreover, a democratic process for reaching an equitable solution to ethnic conflict is not at hand. It is available only after the relevant universe of those entitled to vote has been established—but which ethnic group will be given the right to vote? The human rights approach, whether focused on individual and/or collective rights, will yield unsatisfactory results because it is difficult, if not impossible, to draw a line at which all the rights of the minority are met and none of the rights of the majority are violated.

In sum, resolving ethnic conflict by resort to boundaries, votes, and human rights, whether individual or collective, is not likely to produce a stable solution, given the issues involved. Little wonder that force is used in settling the argument, as in the Yugoslav civil war and elsewhere. It is also not surprising that the logic of national political nihilism is now dominant in many areas of the world caught up in ethnic strife and that in such regions and countries the atmosphere discourages investment.

In no small measure, the poor investment climate in these postcommunist societies can be attributed to the outbursts of nationalistic politics and ethnic strife. With the collapse of the containing structure that the political arrangements of the communist period provided, people are now free to act out ancient grievances. Ethnic hatreds can be kept simmering from generation to generation, providing a reservoir of hostile biases and bitter memories of historic grievances that are shared by members of an ethnic group and can set off active antagonism in times of group hardships or under the prodding of an irresponsible and self-serving leadership. Whatever measures are undertaken to improve the investment climate must take into account the nature of these societies. Potential investors should and will take this into account as well.

## LATIN AMERICA

For all their problems, Latin American countries have achieved respectability among international investors. This is particularly true for managers of specialist emerging-market funds, who control more than $100 billion in assets. Some of these managers have shifted their money from Southeast Asia to Latin America. The equity markets of Argentina, Brazil, Chile, and Mexico probably had a combined market capitalization of more than $500 billion in the mid-1990s. The region's smaller markets, such as Colombia, Peru, and even Venezuela, have done well and continue to attract investors.

There are problems in Latin America. In Argentina, trade unions strongly protest cuts in welfare programs, as indeed they do the world over. Mexico must deal with guerrilla groups in its hinterland. Brazil's landless clash with government authorities. In fact, throughout the region, the poor districts that ring the various Latin American cities are awash with crime, drugs, and general unrest.

*The Economist* has noted that even though many of the problems are unique to the country, there does appear to be a common thread to them all.[4] Except in Chile, more than a decade of roughly democratic regimes, market economies, and low inflation has not produced sustained growth. Such growth as the region has achieved has not been broadly shared among the people. Indeed, for many people, the efforts at privatization, freer trade, and monetary and fiscal stability have meant bankruptcy, unemployment, and cuts in welfare programs.

Thus far, these difficulties have not been freely articulated by the people so impacted nor by their representatives. Populist or authoritarian upheaval does not seem likely. *The Economist* cites a mid-1990s regionwide poll that reports 27 percent of respondents judge their own country's democracy as working well; yet 61 percent still see that as the best form of government.[5]

The fact is that liability and institutions cannot be changed rapidly. This is as true in Latin America as it is in Eastern Europe and elsewhere. The difficulties lie in how to make both governments and markets more efficient and effective. Bloated bureaucracies staffed by poorly trained people are in charge in much the same way as in the prereform period. Lack of properly functioning legal systems, labor, and goods markets conspire to drag down both the economy and the government. The existing systems in place simply do not provide value for the money spent. In sum, these countries should push ahead and complete their macroeconomic reforms and at the same time complement them with the necessary microeconomic and governmental reforms or risk jeopardizing such progress as they have achieved.

It is the appearance that reform, as in Eastern Europe, has stopped short of achieving projected goals that has produced a backlash in the mid-1990s. The great expectations that accompanied reforms have by and large been unrealized. For their part, the various populist and authoritarian leaders have put forward unlikely and unacceptable solutions. The net effect has been disgust with all politics and an upsurge in crime and violence.

Time is not on the side of the reformers as they look for ways to promote growth and speed up the delivery of social benefits to the people. Needless to say, reformers too are frustrated in their efforts. The mix of privatization, market liberalization, and related political reforms has been slow in producing the expected results. In any case, the first wave of reforms were popular as liberalization boosted growth and imports as well as expansion of credit. At the same time, a new political leadership appeared in several of the countries with bold programs of future reforms with promises of more growth.

Unfortunately, these expectations were unrealistic. In Mexico and Venezuela, short-lived booms ended in banking and financial crises. In Brazil and Argentina, developments too were unsatisfactory. The region's traditional gap between incomes widened even though the reforms of the early 1990s reduced poverty, thanks in part to population increases. Unemployment is now higher than in the early 1990s, and real wages have fallen. Estimates now are provided that suggest a stable growth rate of 6 percent will take another decade or more to achieve.

The evidence also suggests, as *The Economist* underscores, that the region's voters may not be willing to wait a decade or more for desired results. In fact, reaction to the International Monetary Fund (IMF) produced a 40 percent vote for the ex-Marxist Sandinistas in Nicaragua. In Venezuela, middle-class reaction at cuts in utility and energy subsidies threw out the country's political leadership in 1993. Some people see their problems as the consequence of too much democracy, particularly problems with the slowness of reforms and the upsurge of crime and violence. The danger is that these issues may well distract the public from the need to build up the courts, an accountable public service, as well as political parties so as to strengthen democracy and avoid the personalization of power.

However, now even influential groups in Washington and elsewhere are arguing that perhaps a strong president is needed in these Latin countries if the necessary reforms are to be carried out and growth promoted. Perhaps political power has been too decentralized and encouraged local politicians to frustrate reforms. Privatization, too, has its downside in many of these countries, it is argued. Measures are needed to contain corruption and abuse at the corporate level. Social spending should be targeted where it is most needed. Currently, such spending is in the largely corrupt centralized bureaucracies. Critics suggest and indeed strongly recommend that social services should be turned over to local governments and nongovernmental agencies to administer.

For all the problems, the leadership in the region seems determined to carry out the necessary reforms. To be sure, their will to do so may well have been reinforced by the international financial community as well, which presents few, if any, alternatives to reform. One can hope that given the backlash to reforms, the authoritarian temptations can be avoided and democracy and growth promoted while preserving a viable social safety net.

Claiming Latin American economies successfully reformed is indeed risky business. Like an addict of the drugs that grow so well there, the region has a history of reform and relapse. How well the region manages to cope with its laundry list of problems will likely determine its future success. Some observers argue that the region's system lends itself easily to corruption. It is a part of the Latin American culture. They note that the Latin American countries were governed for 300 years by viceroys sent by Spain, usually as a reward for some favor done for the Spanish king. Many returned to Spain as rich men. Today it is almost an article of faith that any Latin American with any talent will acquire a fortune before leaving public office.

Some observers note that the extensive conversions by Protestant missionaries taking place in Latin America (and in Africa) may mean that external cultural influences will increasingly have a deep transforming effect on the civilization in these countries. There is the hope of absorbing Latin America into the North American and European orbit not only by religious conversion, but also by such schemes as the North American Free Trade Agreement (NAFTA). They argue that Latin American society can be really and truly Westernized only if populations of Amerindian and African ancestry can enjoy free and easy acceptance among the reigning elites in society. Although they may be correct, the prospects do not seem likely for a long time.

## ASIAN RIM

In some of the emerging markets in Asia, uncertainty over prospects for Hong Kong after China takes over has caused some investors to avoid the former British colony, where the major stock index dropped 30 percent in dollar terms in recent years. For its part, China has promised Hong Kong a high degree of autonomy, to be exercised through Hong Kong's legislature. The facts, however, may be otherwise, since China does not appear to be firmly committed to granting such autonomy. Indeed, China appears to be well on the road to dismantling Hong Kong's elected legislature, so autonomy seems a lost cause.

It was not long ago that Japan served as an example for the world. Japanese management, with its various examples of modernity and success in doing things right, was the benchmark. Times do change. Sophisticated Japanese managers are now, once again, looking at how Western companies are dealing with various managerial and technological problems, including motivating people and tying together various far-flung world operations. The main elements of the Japanese model—consensus building and shared decision making—depend on close physical proximity and shared cultural values and simply do not lend themselves well to global operations.

An appraisal of Japanese efforts in crafting successful policies leaves room for doubt. It is true that the country's interlocking relationships of businesses facilitate the formation and execution of policies to promote trade interests probably better than, for instance, in the United States. The fact is that such efforts by Japan are also crowned by serious failure, as demonstrated in Japan's attempts to promote a civilian air transportation industry. Such an inward-looking trade strategy as Japan's, with its promotion and protection of domestic industries, has come at the expense of the Japanese consumers—at least in the short term.

Other weak and problem areas in Japan in the long and short term are: (1) the troublesome banking system; (2) an aging population, which will require significant increases in resources devoted to social services; and (3) serious shortcomings in the infrastructure as a result of urban growth. Whether the young generation of Japanese is willing to continue the sacrifices required to stay the course of their parents remains an open question. The young generation appears more self-centered and less interested in making such sacrifices.

The slow pace of change in Japan is underscored by the country's so-called vote for reform in October 1996. Disappointing though efforts have been, Japan did manage one significant change in 1996. In the 1980s and early 1990s, government was seen as the solution to most economic and social problems. After 1996, bureaucrats are no longer seen as the solution: they are seen as the problem. Indeed, the Japanese government would be on firmer ground if its bureaucrats  had less discretion and were more accountable, made to act as servants rather than masters as they have for decades.  Nothing short of straightforward deregulation will do the job. In particular, such efforts should be directed at the six most troubled aspects of the economy—finance, telecommunications, employment, distribution, land and housing, and health and welfare.

None of these issues and problems have deterred the Japanese from pushing their model elsewhere in Asia. Japanese experts argue that Japan wants to share the knowledge gleaned from the country's miraculous development, especially with Vietnam and other emerging markets in Asia. After all, they argue that the Vietnamese, like the Japanese, have been influenced by Confucius and value education, discipline, and strong government. There is a rich tradition, in their view, that underpins Asia's postwar success and that Asians, including the Japanese, should take pride in. There is no need for Asians to conform to American rules. Given the demonstrated success of the Japanese model, there is every reason to believe that Japan should help lead a sort of Asian renaissance. In their view, Asia is no longer a place for Westerners to civilize and convert; its prosperity has revived Asia's independent dignity.

Earlier, I discussed the role of culture.  A culture can serve to promote development. It can also sustain local morale and cohesion in times of trouble. The danger is that it may produce a bunker mentality dictating a systematic disregard of, or deliberate inattention to, the ideas and skills alien people and cultures have at their command.  The end result is to be disastrously left behind by the rest of the world. Beginning early in the nineteenth century, even a civilization as vast and successful as the Chinese had to face up to this hard fact.  China has yet to fully recover from failing to do so.

The Japanese experts, in particular, take exception to the criticism leveled at Japan's model by the World Bank and IMF, which they see as propagandists for the American model and the dominant goals of privatization, markets, and price stability.  Such goals, if completely adopted by Asian emerging economies such as Vietnam, will hurt economic growth, undermine popular support for reform, create unemployment, and lead to a loss of the government income that privatization might bring. The experts argue that strong state leadership is especially necessary in a country like Vietnam, where market forces are too rudimentary to be trusted.

Given Asian experience with Japan's coprosperity sphere of the 1930s and early 1940s, it is not clear how receptive the Vietnamese and others will be to Japanese advice and their model. After all, the interventionist Japanese model was easier to follow in the 1960s than in the 1990s, since the industrialized Western countries are less likely to look with favor on trade protection. Moreover, the Vietnamese in particular are more likely to follow the American model and advice, with its emphasis on the development of equity and bond markets. The cash and development programs pushed by the Japanese may matter more to Japan than to Vietnam.

The other East Asian countries (in addition to Japan) usually labeled as Pacific Rim countries are South Korea, Taiwan, Singapore, and Hong Kong. All of them have several characteristics in common with Japan. Except for Japan, all have been created following World War II, and they are all resource poor, as is Japan. They all stress the important role for government of creating, promoting, and executing industrial development and national prosperity. They all, presumably, also share a commitment to free markets while pushing for state assistance to industry. In the cases of South Korea and Taiwan, both use economic planning that is linked to expert development.

For all its problems, India has come a long way down the road to private markets and private investment. The country has undertaken an ambitious program for reform and development of capital markets—a far-reaching program of financial sector reforms, including adoption of internationally accepted prudential norms, interest rate liberalization, revamping of bank supervision, and encouragement of new private banks. At the same time, India has put in place a sustained effort toward macroeconomic stabilization. In fact, the primary issues in the country's stock market have more than tripled between 1991/92 and 1993/94.

The situation is far less satisfactory in Pakistan. Prospects for rational reform and democracy are uncertain at best. Indeed, Islamic fundamentalists wait in the wings—a disquieting prospect, given the chaos in neighboring Afghanistan. In 1996, Pakistan's president intervened to remove the prime minister for corruption and mismanagement. It was the third time since 1990 that such action was taken.

## AFRICA AND EMERGING MARKETS

The failings that have handicapped Africa's efforts at reform are as much political as economic. Thus it is that foreign investors who might otherwise be attracted by Africa's relatively inexpensive labor are deterred by the hassle of dealing in countries where the rules of law are so weak that even simple contracts can be difficult to enforce. Bribes to badly paid bureaucrats are a way of doing business. These bribes, for all practical purposes, constitute an informal welfare system. They also serve to break an obstructive bureaucracy and force firms to pay heavily for doing business in Africa. In fact, the World Bank and International Monetary Fund are reluctant to portray Africa as a loser for fear of scaring away potential investors. They delicately avoid mentioning the word corruption and never use that word in the same breath as the name of an individual country.

Even the continent's relatively best performing economies—English-speaking Ghana and two French-speaking neighbors, Burkina Faso and the Ivory Coast—underscore the legacy of colonialism and the fragmentation that the colonial powers encouraged. This fragmentation is another stumbling block to development in Africa. These three countries are but a case in point. Together they form a natural economic unit whose market, with a total population of 40 million, would begin to make it inviting to foreign investors. Separately, they are poor, small, and isolated markets in which the political reward for outside investors often seems too small to justify the perceived risks of doing business in Africa.

Africa's failure to coalesce can be attributed in good measure to the arbitrary European imposition of borders in the nineteenth century. Many experienced analysts and frustrated business people attribute the costly mistakes made by Africans and their foreign investors to the independence era, which began with Ghana's statehood in 1957. They condemn the rapid transformation of many African countries into predatory states. Many of their governments have simply served to expropriate business and/or impose confiscatory taxes or demand bribes. The political will to make changes does not exist because agents of the state have grown used to using corruption to round out their personal budgets.

At the same time, the outside world has played an important role in continuing the fragmentation of the continent. Prominent here, according to some observers, are the World Bank and IMF. France is the most active of the European countries on the continent and the only former colonial power to have retained its grip on its one-time colonies. The World Bank and other lenders duplicate Africa's fragmentation and ultimately help perpetuate it by organizing their projects on a country-by-country basis.

Moreover, it is only the selfishly defined interests of various ruling political elites reluctant to cede any portion of their sovereignty that impedes progress; it is (in the case of French-speaking Africa) France itself that is reluctant to encourage its former colonies to integrate with English-speaking countries. To a great extent, France's objection to an integrated West Africa of 40 million is that such an economic giant would come to rival France's influence in the region. France worked to dismember Nigeria by actively supporting Biafran secessionists during Nigeria's civil war in the late 1960s. In support of such accusations, businesspeople in West Africa describe different actions by Paris in the region in 1995 aimed at limiting non-French interests in many spheres, be they those of English-speaking Africans or of Westerners.

## AN ISLAMIC RENAISSANCE?

Various campaigns in Africa and elsewhere to move against Muslim militants do not appear to have had much success or attraction for potential investors. In Egypt, for instance, critics of the Muslim Brotherhood have long argued that its leaders have supplied financial and ideological support to an estimated 3,000 underground fighters who have been battling the Egyptian government since 1992. Crackdowns against militant Islamic movements and figures have taken place in many of the North African countries. Egypt has accused the government of Sudan of supporting a failed plot to assassinate President Hosni Mubarak of Egypt in Ethiopia in June 1995.

Consider, for instance, the ongoing tragedy of the 1990s in Algeria. It is, in fact, a battleground where a militant political Islamic movement may seize power. Hundreds of leading figures in Algeria, including intellectuals, politicians (one of them a president), journalists, emancipated women, foreigners, and thousands of ordinary Algerians, have fallen victim to fundamentalist violence. Algeria is important because a militant political Islam will lead to violence.

Recent attempts to "rethink Islam" in a modern mode may not be any more successful than efforts to reform communism, which ultimately led to a dead end. This does not mean, of course, that Islamic revival is a useless exercise. Militant movements so much in the news see as their task mobilization for political action. Their common thread is hostility to the West. The antithesis to their efforts are those calling for integration of Islam with Western cultures. In this view, the task is to revitalize Muslim faith and intellectual culture.

Those experts arguing for revitalization of Islam tend to be highly critical of the past and present conditions of Islamic thought and contemporary Islamic societies, though not always by name.[6] Some people argue, in effect, that the Koran's spiritual transformation power over the hearts and minds of Muslims has been obscured. In their view, the spiritual essence of the covenant between God and people has been allowed to deteriorate into legal codes, rituals, and ideologies of domination in the interest of religious and political elites. Much of the early achievements of Islam have been abandoned long ago. Currently the various Islamic regimes suppress, control, and manipulate Islam simply to remain in power, while Islamic opposition movements, contrary to their claims, actually secularize their societies. Their vocabulary of religious reference is without genuine religious vision. These critics underscore that the best place and prospects for the revival of Islamic culture are in the West, for the simple reason that no Muslim society permits independent intellectual criticism.

In effect, the revival of Islamic culture depends on a Muslim renaissance that would allow for a thinking of the hitherto unthought in Islam. This would require a revival of the philosophic, scientific, and humanistic culture of Islam's classical period and assimilation of the industrial and information revolutions with Islam's modern social, scientific, theological, and philosophical insights. This is nothing less than putting in place an intellectual apparatus essential to a critical formulation of an Islam modernity—an overwhelming task indeed, but if it is not undertaken and successful, Islam will be in a form that is communalist, separatist, and parochial.

It is not at all clear whether such a national, ethical, and individualistic vision of Islam will satisfy those who respond to militant political Islamic movements. It may, however, appeal to the few and perhaps to the Muslim populations of modernized industrial societies. The problem is that Islam can claim few such societies. More typical of Islamic societies are uprooted peoples deprived of such elementary rights as political participation, education, employment, and adequate health and housing facilities. Little wonder that such people are easy prey for militant political Islamic movements.

## NOTES

1. See George Macesich, *Transformation and Emerging Markets* (Westport, CT: Praeger, 1996).

2. See Celestine Bohlen, "A Marxist Splinter Party Maintains Influence in Italy," *New York Times*, Tuesday, December 17, 1996, p. A6.

3. See "Tigers or Tortoises?" *The Economist* 341, no. 7989, October 26, 1996, p. 98.

4. See "The Backlash in Latin America," *The Economist* 341, no. 7994, November 30, 1996, pp. 19–21.

5. Ibid.

6. See, for instance, Mohammed Arkoun, *Common Question, Uncommon Answers*, translated and edited by Robert D. Lee (Boulder, CO: Westview Press, 1994). See also Ira Milapidus, "Islam without Militance," *New York Times Book Review*, August 21, 1996, pp. A9–10.

# 6

# Issues of Economic Growth

## A RETURN TO CLASSICAL ECONOMICS?

The collapse of central planning in the Eastern European countries (and elsewhere) and the dramatic rise of countries on the Asian rim has again raised the issue of why some countries grow successfully and others do not. On this issue the Keynesian research program or paradigm does not yield useful insights. Its orientation is toward short-term changes in total spending, which takes as a given the structure of economic institutions. The classical research program and economists from Adam Smith on is a more promising source, since the classics focus on the slow but persistent changes in the economy.

Briefly, classical economists focused on the growth aspects of capital accumulation. They stressed the ongoing transformation of labor into capital as a distinguishing characteristic of a market-oriented capitalist economy. Adam Smith and David Ricardo, among others, emphasized the growth aspects of capital accumulation. Karl Marx, for his part, focused on the creation of private accumulation of wealth and its class aspects.

According to Smith, growth is the direct result of the division of labor, widening markets, and accumulation of capital. In particular, Smith's key to growth is the accumulation of capital that is collected from savings. Accumulation allows greater labor specialization and widening of markets. The whole process, in his view, depends upon the security of property. As this process moves the economy forward to higher levels, so too is the social order elevated. The process maintains an orderly market equilibrium that assures a pattern of production fitted to demand. Together with a system of natural liberty, an equilibrium of forces is produced, which moves the entire economy to even greater wealth.

The classical economists picked up Smith's analytical system, including equilibrium of supply and demand in competition markets and the labor theory of value, and pushed forward analysis of economic and policy problems. Most economists who followed in Smith's tradition tended to favor freedom for economic enterprise and limited government. They also accepted Smith's liberalism and his system of natural liberty.

Foremost was David Ricardo, writing in the first quarter of the turbulent nineteenth century. He was a strong advocate of capital accumulation. In his view, the growth of capital was the sole source of economic growth. Ricardo argued that economic freedom led to maximum profits, which were the source of investment capital, and a competitive economy would lead to profit-maximizing investments. In short, public policies that benefitted businesses would lead to maximum economic growth.

There is general agreement that Ricardo's theory encouraged governments to keep their distance from economic and business affairs, which were best left to private businesspeople. If left alone, the economy would achieve the maximum growth possible. Ricardian economics, at least in the second-rate minds of the mass of its adherents, served to promote business interests and a favorable public policy for many years.

This is not surprising. Ricardo was first of all a businessman—a stockbroker—who made a fortune early in life, retired from business, bought a country estate, and went into public life. Unlike Adam Smith, whose work nevertheless taught him much, Ricardo was no wide-ranging and thorough, "bookish" scholar, and had no well-meditated and articulate, all-embracing social and moral philosophy. Nevertheless, Ricardo was an active member of England's Parliament, the country's leading expert in its problems of economic policy, and a very sophisticated economic theorist. And, unlike Smith, whose work is rich in realistic details but lacks theoretical precision and rigor, Ricardo's work never mentions any specific facts but is all pure, rigorous abstract theory, underscoring his ability to focus on essential, general principles.

Although Ricardo was firmly attached to the "economic liberalism" that had been supported earlier by the Physiocrats, Adam Smith, and others, he was objective enough as a theorist to adhere to his logic, and assumptions led him to a set of conclusions that on the whole were rather more pessimistic than optimistic and must have been very disappointing. In good measure, Ricardo created a theoretical system of which some main elements were to aid Karl Marx—who indeed changed what he took from Ricardo, developed it in his own way, and added much else of his own to provide "scientific proof" that socialism, not economic liberalism, is destined to become the only regime able to meet the needs of mankind and survive.

To be sure, the elements of Ricardo's system that Marx built upon has historic connections, but the Marxist account of the matter exaggerates the degree of resemblance and logical connection between the two systems. Of course, the proponents of "economic liberalism" may well have been seriously infected with a liberal-optimistic bias. They stressed the harmonious and generally beneficial aspects of the potential functioning and development of "free" or unfettered competitive capitalism. They also tended to downplay the system's weaknesses, disharmonies, and internal difficulties.

On the other hand, the Marxists were even more infected with the bias of the opposite, extremely pessimistic view of capitalism, and blind to the good features of market capitalism promoted by liberal economists. Marxist theory does yield insights into the features of capitalism that account for both its dynamism and its difficulties or tendencies to develop malfunctionings endangering its power to endure as a system. The Marxist insights into all this both stand alone and grossly exaggerate it so as to produce the desired proof that the capitalist system is fated to destroy itself and, in dying, give birth to the world's predestined, eventual socialist utopia. Ricardo, however, in about equal measures of contrast with most other liberal economists and with Marx, was perhaps no enthusiastic optimist about the system he favored and viewed as the relatively best and most possible one in his world and time. Nonetheless, he was objective and able to carry on and develop the line of thought and insights in the liberal tradition and to go part of the way toward the very different and later views and insights of Karl Marx. Indeed, Ricardo supplied much of the valid part as well as the invalid part of Marxist thought.

In Marx's view, capitalism (a term he invented) is doomed. His demonstration of its demise draws in so-called laws of creation of capitalist society. On one level Marx bases his argument on the inherent injustices of capitalism that lead ultimately to economic and social conditions that cannot be maintained.  At another level his argument is sociological, in that class conflict between increasingly affluent capitalists and the increasingly miserable working class will break out in social revolution.  At still another level the argument is economic, in that accumulation of capital in private hands, while creating increasing abundance, also leads to the inevitable breakdown in capitalism.  At all three levels the idea of conflict is underscored: conflict between the ideal and reality—the moral issue; conflict between labor and capital—the sociological issue; and conflict between growth and stagnation—the economic issue.  This conflict generates change, and so capitalism, according to Marx, must eventually give way to another social system in which conflict is replaced by ethical, social, and economic harmony.  This change is the "dialectical process" whereby socialism will replace capitalism.  Thus Marx created one of the world's most powerful ideologies, whose vision of abundance, equality, and freedom stood in challenge to classical-liberal individualism, private property, and private enterprise.

The rise of socialism, the demand for social justice, and Marx's use of such instruments of the dominant ideology as the labor theory of value and the theory of capital accumulation to attack its legitimacy—all prompted a search for a theoretical defense of the existing system.  In part, the new defense presented is that of the philosophy of the individual developed and cultivated largely by dominant business and economic interests in the midnineteenth century up to and beyond World War II.  In effect, it is a reinforced version of the familiar laissez-faire argument long known to scholars.

Economists for the most part did not take the extreme position of individualism and laissez-faire very seriously.  For one thing, Benthamite utilitarianism (Jeremy Bentham, 1748–1832) suggested that government intervention may on occasion be justified by the greatest-good argument.  For another, economists concerned themselves with pressing social issues for which the philosophy of extreme individualism provided little insight.  This did not mean, however, that economists rejected the individualist philosophy.  On the contrary, they remained within its general framework.

More important, economists intentionally or otherwise developed a new theoretical apparatus that presumably serves to refute the Marxist critique of capitalism.  This is the neoclassical economics developed since 1870.  In effect, the foundation of economics is reduced to the desires and wants of the individual, and the whole theoretical explanation of production, distribution, and prices is based on the single assumption of rational individual self-interest. Neoclassical economics is a significant scientific advance, since it reduces to the simple but elegant idea of marginalism a complex set of separate theories of value, distribution, and returns to factors of production. The value of a product or service is not the result of the amount of labor embodied in it, but of the usefulness of the last unit purchased. With marginalism a new approach to economics developed.

Of course, the world economy has changed over the years since classical economics became popular. Nevertheless, the fundamental relationships between population, accumulation of capital, technology, and economic growth that are central concerns of classical economics are today also the concern of economic policy. It should be no surprise that today economists and policy makers are turning to insights provided by classical economics.

As we discussed, Thomas S. Kuhn noted that the crises leading to paradigm shifts often begin with new discoveries, experimental discrepancies that cannot be squeezed into the established framework. In the case of classical economics, useful insights continue to be provided, underscoring our earlier discussion of the importance of historical experience in knowledge building in economics. Unlike Kuhn's paradigm shift in classical economics, there is no tearing down and reassembling the pieces into something quite new. It is more like an act of construction bound to social forces and constrained by habits and biases. Economists would do well to study history and understand their discipline in its historical setting.

As we noted, Keynesian macroeconomics is unable to deal with persistent changes in the economy. This can be attributed in good measure to its orientation toward short-term changes in total spending together with the assumption of a given structure of economic institutions. To be sure, the post–World War II boom kept the economy dynamic and unemployment relatively low through the 1950s. By the 1970s the great postwar boom gave way to relative stagnation. It became clear that the process of economic growth itself created problems of unemployment and low incomes deep within the structure of capitalist market-oriented economies. It also became clear that simple Keynesian economics and policies were inadequate to deal with these issues. Whether capitalist market-oriented economies can survive without growth or with slow growth became a singularly important issue, and prompted many economists and policy makers to examine growth-related issues long discussed by classical economists.

The road to a revived classical (or neoclassical) research program focused not only on microeconomics but on monetary microeconomics as well. We have discussed the essence of the program at some length in our earlier discussion of Milton Friedman's contributions. Friedman advocates the virtues of a competitive private-enterprise, economy, although he also stresses the need for government to establish a framework within which the free market can function more effectively. In these efforts, for many years he included the contributions of Henry C. Simons and Frank Knight at the University of Chicago, as well as others who provide the cornerstone of the Chicago School.

Friedman provides an important extension of the classical liberal philosophy that goes back to Adam Smith and classical economics. He argues that the operation of a free market and noninterventionist government policy yield far more desirable results than would otherwise be obtained by restricting the market's operation.

We have discussed his views on fiscal policy and monetary policy. He has revived and given life to the quantity theory of money by showing that the monetary system affects the level of aggregate demand and the national output in a wide variety of subtle ways. In particular, he discusses an active monetary policy promoted by money Keynesians as a source of considerable mischief and in any case counterproductive. His advice is for a steady and gradual increase in a country's money supply as an aid to economic expansion and growth. Money is indeed important. Instability in the monetary system has always been the chief cause of instability in employment and output. Stabilize the monetary system, and economic stability will follow.

## GROWING THE ECONOMY AND SOCIETY

The importance and sources of economic growth, as we see, attract considerable attention. Economic growth is taken to mean a sustained increase in per capita or per worker product, most often accompanied by an increase in population and usually by sweeping structural changes.[1] Such growth may come about because of capital formation, by continuing improvements in techniques in products. Other sources include receipt of income from a rich national resource such as oil, decision of an increased share of the population to enter the labor force, decision to work more hours per week, or, in densely populated countries, a catastrophe that decreases the population, leaving more resource's per person.

The appeal of classical theory on the growth issue is illustrated in the instance of technological change and capital formation. Adam Smith was very much concerned with technological change. In his view technological progress consisted of increase in the division of labor. His successors, however, gradually turned their attention away from technological change so that by limiting the complexity of their analysis, they could reason with some certainty about the remaining factors. By the time of the Alfred Marshall and his *Principles of Economics,* this approach was generally accepted. Indeed, in most contributions to neoclassical economic theory from Alfred Marshall to J. M. Keynes and later there is an explicit statement to the effect that the state of the arts is held as a constant—in effect, that there is an absence of any advance in technological knowledge. This simplification enabled the analyst to focus on the remaining problems. Those problems included questions on relative prices, competition and monopoly in the production and distribution of goods and services, international economic relations, the distribution of income, the level of employment, and inflation. Great advances in these areas have been made by economists. In making these advances, economists have taken into account the effects of technological change. In their formal theory, however, technological change as such is not included.

One consequence of the exclusion of technological change from the formal body of neoclassical economic theory is that income per capita rises only because of capital formation. In effect, economists and others have applied capital formation to economic growth as the only source of rise in per capita income. They have neglected to carry forward Smith's analysis of technological change by assuming it away. Economists have taken a wrong turn in the road in applying their analysis and conclusions to reality without recalling the assumptions and analytical framework on which the conclusions are based.

Technological change has been with us for centuries, and increases in per capita income have been occurring everywhere. If we had data extending back in time for thousands of years, we would very likely see that the human standard of living has improved between each of two given points. The long-term rising trend has been slow until recent years.

We also know that geographically some countries have done better than others in terms of growth. Economic growth is universal among countries in Europe and North America, less common in Latin America, and least discernible in many countries of Asia and Africa. There is evidence that the pace of growth has picked up since the 1980s even in the hitherto lagging countries.

When we ask what this technological progress is that is the cause of rising increase, a number of answers are suggested. First is the discovery of new knowledge, which makes possible an increase in the output of goods and services per unit of labor, capital, and materials used in production. The second is the incorporation of such knowledge into the productive processes. It includes new products and services as well as new methods of production. All of the processes of innovation in the arts, sciences, technology, and organization are involved. Economists call all these varied activities "technological progress." Their common link is the devising of new concepts.

Of course, incomes may rise even in the absence of technological progress. It may do so, for instance, because of capital formation that is the product of additional instruments of production. And as we note earlier, income may also increase owing to sale of a natural resource such as oil, an increase in hours worked by the labor force, or, indeed, a catastrophe that decreases the population, leaving more resources per person. Nevertheless, if capital formation consists only of the construction of tools and machines and so forth that do not embody new ideas, the rise in income will gradually end. If economic growth and so income is to continue to rise, continuing improvement in technology, products, and services must take place.

Most economists now agree that economic growth is the product of the accelerating cumulation of scientific and technological knowledge.[2] Most people will also agree that the major source of such knowledge spread from the West and provided the main source of change in Latin America, Asia, and Africa during modern times. In fact, most social scientists would agree that except for Western intrusion and example, the social structure and techniques that characterized traditional societies would be little changed even in the twentieth century. Clearly, most societies desire income, wealth, and power. Technological progress promises all three.

The historical facts do not explain the pace of knowledge over the centuries. Thus some ancient Greeks knew that the earth is not the center of the universe. How is that when the advance of knowledge began again, the same knowledge was not reached again until the seventeenth century? The reason for the slow pace may well be found in the traditional societies based on peasant agriculture.[3] Other hypotheses suggest that some countries have achieved faster or greater economic progress than others because of race, religion, geography, climate, personality, resistances to cultural change, or economic conditions. As a matter of fact, it may well be that some of these hypotheses may add to our understanding of economic growth. These hypotheses should be accepted not in some absolute sense, but only in the sense that they may be consistent with available data and may well be repeated as new or additional evidence becomes available.

Such evidence as we do have suggests that the economic state of a society is closely related to its political state, and forces that bring about change in one also bring some sort of change in the other. A society whose technology is unchanging, for instance, is unchanging in other elements of its culture as well. Hagen argues, probably correctly, that lack of consistent progress in techniques is a characteristic of all traditional societies and only of traditional societies, except that during a period when forces for change are disrupting traditional societies, technological change may become evident before social-political change becomes overt, or the reverse may be true.[4]

He stresses that the historical record underlying his generalization is complex because of the pressure in modern times of colonialism under which the political forms were neither traditional nor modern, but rather imposed and not representative of the indigenous social structure beneath. He argues that the broad generalization is seen if one notes that the period preceding the Industrial Revolution is also the period of the divine right of kings, and when the technically unprogressive societies of America, Asia, and Africa were conquered by Europeans, all were traditional.

So it is that economic growth occurs rather gradually and over a considerable period of time. Contact with technologically advanced societies is a necessary condition for rapid technological progress, though such progress does not occur only because of this contact. The innovations required are not only technoeconomic, but social as well. Indeed, the latter may be even more complex. Major political and social changes occur during the processes of economic growth. Whatever the causes of such growth, they most surely impact on many aspects of human behavior.

Another contribution to the various attempts to gain insights into the processes of economic growth is that of W. W. Rostow.[5] His conception of economic growth attracted considerable attention at the time. According to Rostow, a society moving to economic growth passes from a traditional stage through four added stages, those of developing the preconditions for take-off, the take-off, the drive to maturity, and high mass-consumption.

A traditional society, according to Rostow, is one in which methods of production are limited, the view of the world is pre-Newtonian, a high proportion of productive resources is devoted to agriculture, there is little vertical social mobility, and the value system is fatalistic.

The preconditions period is the period when the idea spreads that economic progress is possible and good; education broadens and changes; new enterprising people appear; banks appear; investment increases, particularly in communication, transportation, and the extraction of raw materials; the scope of commerce widens; and an occasional manufacturing establishment appears. Three changes are especially important: creation of an effective national government, an increase in agricultural productivity, and establishment of a substructure of social overhead capital.

The period of take-off, according to Rostow, is the decisive interval in the history of a society when growth becomes its normal condition, the interval when old blocks and resistances to steady growth are finally overcome. All three of the following conditions must occur: a use in the rate of investment, the development of one or more manufacturing sectors of substantial size with a rapid rate of growth, and the quick emergence or existence of a favorable political structure. Income flows into the hands of persons who save and invest a high fraction of it, the economy probably also becomes an attractive place for the investment of foreign capital, the number of entrepreneurs expands, and insofar as they have done so during the previous stage, people become prepared to accept a new way of life.

He notes that the pattern of growth of any new industry is one of rapid expansion and then deceleration; this, he argues, continues to be the pattern throughout later stages. An industry that expands provides stimulus both to industries that provide the capital goods and raw materials it needs (a backward linkage) and to those that use its new or now cheaper products (a forward linkage). Such an industry may be termed a leading sector. The take-off, argues Rostow, occurs within a decade or two or at least within a quarter century or several decades.

A drive to technological maturity follows the take-off. It occupies about sixty years from the time take-off begins. Maturity is the stage at which an economy has the technological versatility to produce as it chooses to.

At some time after it has reached maturity, a nation enters upon the age of high mass consumption. An identifying indicator of this stage is that durable consumer goods and services become more important among the leading sectors. A society that has reached this stage may choose among the pursuit of external power and influence, the development of a welfare state, and further increase in levels of consumption. Western societies, stressing consumption rather than production, have allocated increased amounts of resources for social welfare and security.

Rostow notes in his discussion of the stages that in some respects one shades into the next; the lines are perhaps less sharp than is suggested here. The emphasis of his discussion, however, is on contrasting characteristics of the several stages, as of course it must be if the concept of stages is to have meaning.

The appeal of Rostow's idea is that there is first a period when conditions for growth are established, then one or two decades within which certain distinctive and necessary transitional events begin and are completed, and thereafter, self-sustained continuing growth. Whether or not Rostow's idea of stages of development is correct, it does have attractive features and provocative suggestions. Thus far, however, the empirical evidence to support Rostow's stages is lacking.

One of the leading economists of economic growth, Kuznets, discusses the role of innovation, both technological and social, and provides insights on the interplay of forces that underlie economic growth and structure.[6] Particularly significant is his presentation and discussion of the concept of the economic epoch. By economic epoch he means a relatively long period extending well over a century possessing distinctive characteristics that give it unity and differentiate it from epochs that precede or follow it.[7] He notes that an epochal innovation may be described as a major addition to the stock of human knowledge that provides the potential for sustained economic growth. It is an addition so major that its exploitation and utilization absorb the energies of human societies and dominate their growth for a period long enough to constitute an epoch in economic history.

Examples of such epochs, according to Kuznets, would be the epoch of "merchant capitalism" in Western Europe. The period covers well over two and a half centuries, extending from the end of the fifteenth to the second half of the eighteenth century. It is characterized by the innovation of a breakthrough by Western Europe to the New World. The effect of this breakthrough led to a very large and important increase in the stock of useful knowledge and to its exploitation, and was itself a consequence of improvements in science and technology, bearing upon navigation, ships, and weapons, and of advances in domestic production and political organization. It is the interplay of technological and institutional changes, argues Kuznets, that is the essence of the economic growth that takes place within the framework constituted by some epochal innovation.

Applying his concept of epochal innovation to the modern period or the last two hundred years, Kuznets argues that the epochal innovation that is being exploited is the extended application of science to the problems of economic production. By science he means the study of observable and testable characteristics of the physical world in accordance with the standards of validity accepted by scientists. In essence, he suggests that science-based technology and the broad views needed for its successful exploitation by human societies were so dominant in the countries that sustained modern economic growth as to constitute a distinctive feature of the modern epoch.

To be sure, Kuznets argues, we are still in the midst of this epoch. We can distinguish its basic features; the final shape of the epoch, however, is still hidden from us. Nevertheless, the broad views of the modern epoch can be suggested by three terms: secularism, egalitarianism, and nationalism. He takes secularism to mean concentration in life on earth, with a scale of priorities that assigns a high rank to economic attainment within an acceptable framework of social institutions. It is the secular outlook that is a distinctive characteristic of societies that have participated in modern economic growth, and it can be considered an indispensable accompaniment of modern economic growth. Egalitarianism shifted the bases of social prestige and political power and contributed greatly to economic growth by inducing a much larger flow of talent and energy into economic rather than other pursuits. Nationalism varies greatly in intensity and shows no strong correlation with economic development, although it is certainly present in the organization of the world during the modern economic epoch.

Kuznets does not disagree with Rostow on the value and legitimacy of attempts to suggest some pattern of order in the modern economic growth experience of different countries. On the contrary, he shares Rostow's view on the need to go beyond qualitative and quantitative description to the use of the evidence for a large number of countries and long periods, in combination with analytical tools and imaginative hypotheses, to suggest and explain not only some common patterns but also the major deviations from them. Kuznets does disagree with the sequence of stages Rostow suggests. For instance, the characterization of one stage of growth as self-sustained, and others, by implication, lacking that property, requires substantive analysis not provided in Rostow's study.

It is interesting that Rostow presents his analysis as an alternative to Marx's theory of modern history. And indeed there are some similarities between Rostow's analysis and Marx's stages of development of society. Both are attempts to interpret the evolution of whole societies from an economic perspective; both recognize that economic change has social, political, and cultural consequences.

There are also fundamental differences. The basic Marxian problems of class conflict, exploitation, and inherent stresses within the capitalist process find no place in Rostow's analysis. Nor does Rostow reduce the complexities of people to a single economic dimension, as does Marx. On the contrary, Rostow recognizes that in terms of human motivation many of the most profound economic changes must be viewed as the consequence of noneconomic human motives and aspirations.

## NOTES

1.   See Simon Kuznets, *Modern Economic Growth: Rate, Structure and Spread* (New Haven: Yale University Press, 1967), p. 1.

2.   For instance, see Everett E. Hagen, *On the Theory of Social Change* (Homewood, IL: The Dorsey Press, 1962).

3.   Ibid., p. 16.

4.   Ibid., pp. 25–26 and chapter 4.

5.   See W. W. Rostow, *The Stages of Economic Growth* (Cambridge, England: Cambridge University Press, 1960).

6.   Kuznets.

7.   Ibid., p. 2.

# 7

## A Challenge to American Hegemony

### AMERICAN INFLUENCE

The American economy remains strong even though confronted with some serious problems. A number of these problems are structural and so do not lend themselves readily to easy solutions. Contrary to a widely accepted view, the American economy remains positioned to lead the world in ideas, services, and products.

Indeed, it is with good reason that an appropriate model for other countries may be the American capital market. The legal protection; the requirement of disclosure; the variety of financial instruments available to investors, including stocks, bonds, mutual funds, options, and futures; and the technical capacities of the system all suggest standards that are lacking in needy countries. Such standards of local capital markets are to be connected in a satisfactory manner with global markets. The capital necessary to finance reasonable rates of growth worldwide is simply beyond the capacities of any single country, either from public or private funds. World growth thus requires efficient and effective capital markets in all countries to provide for and sustain the fourth wave of international integration.[1]

Many countries fall far short of guaranteeing domestic and international investors the kinds of protection now given by American securities legislation. For instance, the European Community has made attempts in this direction and encourages regulation to protect investors.

How far such efforts have to go is suggested by the case of Germany, in which it was not until 1994 that legislation was introduced requiring higher disclosure standards, more adequate protection for minority shareholders, and severe penalties for insider trading. In fact, in 1994 Daimler-Benz was the only major German company to adopt the accounting standards that have been a basic requirement of American securities laws for years if a firm is to be listed on the New York Stock Exchange.

With the collapse of the Soviet Union and other socialist states and their subsequent transition to market economies, the American capital market experience has much to offer. This experience is not lost on the Russian stock market, where securities regulators have made a public effort to iron out key infrastructure problems, such as independent registries and a centralized depositary system that had kept investors at bay. A number of Russian companies have now also issued American depositary receipts (shares sold in foreign countries backed by domestic stock) that let foreign investors get a feel for investing in Russia.

Clearly, the Russian capital and securities market has a long way to go to become a viable operation. For instance, the opaque nature of the securities market is suggested in the close of the Russian gas concern RDA Gazprom. Its natural gas production is more than the combined production of the next sixteen largest gas producers. Its 1.53 billion cubic meters of daily output in 1995 was seven and a half times that of the number two producer, Royal Dutch/Shell Groups, and nine times that of the biggest U.S. gas producer, Exxon.

Gazprom has large reserves of some 32 trillion cubic meters at the end of 1995. Royal Dutch/Shell had about 1.5 trillion cubic meters and Exxon over 1 trillion. Nevertheless, the company has now put out an audited profit and loss statement. We have only a vague idea of what the company is worth. Of the more than 23 billion shares, the nearly 2 percent owned abroad trade at $2.18, and the Russian-owned ones go for about 37 cents, for a total of approximately more than 9 billion. Analysts estimate that if investors were to put the same value on Gazprom's reserves as on, say, British Gas's, Gazprom would have a market cap in the trillions of dollars. Indeed, some analysts describe Gazprom as the Saudi Arabia of the world gas industry. Other analysts note that it has always been a company secret who owns its shares and what price it charges for the gas.

American leadership is underscored in the Mexican crisis that erupted in December 1994, when Mexico devalued the peso as foreign reserves evaporated. Unable to borrow, it was days away from default. The United States offered Mexico up to a $20 billion loan. The IMF and other multilateral and foreign lenders offered an additional $30 billion.

By 1997 Mexico managed to repay its debt to the United States and the international lenders three years ahead of schedule. Indeed, the United States managed to turn a $580 million profit on the loan, the difference between what the U.S. Treasury charged Mexico and what the Treasury pays to borrow. So satisfied are the United States and its friends that they have taken steps to insure that the next time a country faces default, it can readily turn to the IMF and a new pool of more than $25 billion as the credit available for such an event.

Some idea of the strength and flexibility of the American economy can be had by a comparison with Japan, the world's other leading economy. Like its American counterpart, the Japanese economy staggered into the 1990s trying to shake off the effects of a global recession. But unlike America, Japan never bounced back: between 1992 and 1996, the American economy, adjusted for inflation, has grown 22 percent, while Japan managed to grow 6 percent. In America, four years of economic stagnation would have generated great suffering. In Japan, unemployment remained below 4 percent, and outrageous social problems, if existent, are well disguised. Always admired for its adaptability and flexibility, Japan has managed to snare itself in the slow-growth syndrome one associates with Britain in the 1960s and 1970s.

To some observers, Japan's poor performance is to be expected. The strong Japanese currency, the yen, made the country's products far less competitive in world markets, while the bureaucracy poorly forecasts sapped business confidence. To these problems may be added those of the banking system, where inadequate provisions were in place for a comprehensive solution, including money for a needed bailout owing in large measure to bad real estate debts. Thanks to stock market losses that have further depressed the net worth of banks, they are reluctant to lend money. This is particularly significant in Japan; since the country lacks an active bond and stock market, Japan depends on banks for credit creation.

To other observers, Japan's problems may well force the country to make serious efforts and deregulate the economy. This is all the more important since traditional fiscal and monetary measures cannot be counted on to combat recessions. Deregulation of the economy may help the country, but it may be an inadequate substitute for effective macroeconomic policies. Whatever reforms Japan finally undertakes, few democracies would allow the likes of the country's corruption-ridden and incompetent Liberal Democratic Party to influence the political processes.

Indeed, Asia's economic miracle, so fashionable to discuss and cite as a success story, leaves something to be desired. To be sure, economic growth has flowed down from Japan to Hong Kong, Singapore, Taiwan, and South Korea, then to Malaysia and Indonesia, and will ultimately flow to China and Vietnam. In a sense, the experience is similar to that in Europe and the United States, but much faster. It took the United States more than half a century, beginning in 1840, to double per capita output. China, on the other hand, has managed to so in a decade after 1978.

Of course, Asian progress and economic growth are visible. Urban development, consumer products, and services appear to be sprouting all over the Asian landscape. It is, nevertheless, important to keep Asian development and progress in proper perspective. After all, China's Gross Domestic Product (GDP) is probably about one-half of Great Britain's in 1995. In fact, Great Britain's GDP is probably larger than those of Hong Kong, Thailand, Malaysia, Indonesia, Singapore, the Philippines, and India combined. According to estimates provided by the International Monetary Fund (IMF), Asia in the 1990s is simply reestablishing the 30 percent of world output it held in 1900. If Asian economic growth rates of the 1990s continue, then Asian economies may be larger than those of America and Europe by about 2020, assuming that population growth in Asia does not overtake favorable economic developments.

In any case, Asian economic success is not shared by all countries in the area. North Korea and Burma (Myanmar), among others, leave much to be desired in terms of not only economic success but political success as well. The countries within Asia are not identical. It is very difficult indeed to include all these countries in one collective. Sooner or later economic growth and the opening of markets will push the laggards into more accountable and participative governments. It is not necessary to deny the universality of human rights to uphold Asian values. After all, Japan, for all its problems, is both very modern and very Japanese.

It was access to American markets and European markets that made Asian prosperity possible. Protectionism in America and Europe would almost certainly have stopped Asian economic progress in its tracks. It is with good reason that responsible world states now should press on with liberalizing trade under the umbrella of the World Trade Organization (WTO).

For the United States, it is also good policy not to confuse trade and politics. Much pressure exists in the United States to extract trade concessions or use trade embargos and threats to secure political goals, including improvements in human rights. For reasons well known, politics and trade cannot be separated into neat compartments. Nevertheless, failure to distinguish between the two risks incoherence and failure to progress with either set of objectives.

Equally important, the United States should not allow itself to be muzzled over human rights by threats over limited access to markets by the country's more odious trading partners, including China. Certainly it would be most unfortunate for the United States to be played off against Europe or any other country for, say, trade with China. Indeed, the very countries who have least compromised their stand on human rights and trade have seen their trade with China expand. Thus the United States has recorded the fastest export trade growth since 1978, when China began its historic opening. For all their cordiality in political relations with China, Great Britain and Germany, for instance, have seen their shares of the Chinese market drop.

The other major economic powers, including Germany and members of the European Union, do not appear positioned to challenge the American role in world economic and political affairs. Germany, for instance, is confronted with serious economic problems, especially unemployment, which in early 1997 registered more than 12.5 percent. The country's labor costs, moreover, are among the world's highest. It is thus not surprising that prospects for reducing unemployment are not particularly great.

Indeed, Germany expects to see significant manufacturing production shifted abroad in the remainder of the 1990s. Much of the shift in such production will favor Eastern European countries. The growing shift abroad in German production and investment is considered by many observers as a threat to the German model and its consensus system, which seeks to maintain social harmony through a sharing of responsibility by government, business, and unions. Thanks to very liberal unemployment benefits and a strong cultural barrier against the creation of low-paying and casual jobs, Germany may well have few options in reducing unemployment.

There may be serious consequences for the European Union, owing to continentwide growth in unemployment. Germans and others concerned about jobs may well seek scapegoats. They may start to draw conclusions that the German drive for a single European currency has placed them in a squeeze. All of this has intruded upon Germany's clubby all–political party reluctance to question monetary union. If it can be achieved only with significant political and social friction, many Germans and Europeans believe that the whole idea of monetary union should be dropped.

A possible solution is to drop the idea of a single currency and fixed exchange rate and tie the European Union together at the economic level with flexible exchange rates. Such an arrangement is especially suitable when a common market is to consist of culturally, linguistically, and economically disparate members. It would permit each member to develop its economy within the confines of its territory, according to its own appraisal of possibilities. Flexible exchange rates provide an "automatic" trade-balancing mechanism, thereby eliminating the necessity for exchange and trade controls. At the same time, the individual nations are freed from leaving to coordinate monetary and fiscal policies and economic development programs with other nations. As a consequence, the chances for a successful common market and so a European Union are improved.

A system of flexible exchange rates would also help compensate for the "stickiness" of wages and prices brought about by different stages of economic development among the member states of a common market. By promoting what would partially deputize for competitive price flexibility, flexible exchange rates would increase the effectiveness of the price mechanism and thus contribute to legitimate economic integration. Such an arrangement provides a means for combining interdependence among member countries through trade with the greatest possible amount of internal monetary and fiscal independence. No member country would be able to impose its policy mistakes on others, nor could it have their mistakes imposed on itself. Each country would be free to pursue policies for internal stability according to its own appraisal of possibilities. If all member countries succeeded in their internal policies, reasonably stable exchange rates would prevail. Effective intercountry coordination would be achieved without the risks of formal but ineffective coordination.

On the other hand, critics of a system of flexible exchange rates argue that an exchange rate left to find its own level will not necessarily trace out an optimum path through time. However, an optimum path is very difficult to define since its criteria hinge on medium-term and long-term expectations, which can never be guaranteed. Nevertheless, there is no necessity that the market per se will come up with a reasonably satisfactory rate. Moreover, in small, undiversified, and less-developed countries, which may be markers of the common market, a lack of sophisticated individuals with a heterogeneous outlook and sufficient capital may impair the working of a competitive market in foreign exchange.

Another criticism is that exchange rate adjustments will not necessarily insulate the level of domestic activity while correcting an interval balance. Exchange rate adjustments are particularly desirable when price levels have curved out of line. The exchange rate correction will restore the terms of trade to their original position and leave the value and balance of trade and real income in each country at their original levels. The units of measurement will simply be changed. This is no longer true where the sources of disturbance are structural changes in trading regions, different rates of full employment growth in several regions joined in a common market, and cyclical income fluctuations. Repercussions on domestic employment and output can be reduced, but they apparently cannot be eliminated by flexible exchange rates.

The case for flexible exchange rates, however, appears to gather strength in a multinational common market, in which labor immobility caused by cultural differences exists or a central government does not exist—or if it does exist, is indifferent or incapable of assuming responsibility for easing a depressed or less-developed region's adjustments. It may be just such a case that recent writers have in mind when they argue that if a common market is divided into national regions, and if within each factor there is mobility and between factors there is immobility, then each region can have a separate currency that fluctuates relative to all other currencies. In this case, the national region as an economic unit and the currency domain coincide. Moreover, the stabilization argument for flexible exchange rates is valid when based on regional currency areas.

In essence, the basic monetary problem in a common market arises from the fact that there are two or more sovereign governments, while there can only be one source of money creation in a common market with fixed exchange rates. If the government of either Country A or Country B, for example, lowers or raises expenditures, borrowing the difference from its own banks or from the central banks, both countries may suffer inflationary consequences, while only the first government gets what it buys with the money. If one of the countries uses budgetary policy in a conscious and responsible way to combat inflation, it may find itself continually raising taxes and cutting its budget, while the other country, which is causing the inflation by lowering taxes and in general increasing its expenditures, is deriving the benefits. The monetary system and banking system, in effect, constitute a pool of purchasing power available to the governments of the several member countries. An understanding must be reached on how the members will share the available purchasing power.

Such an arrangement must be capable of coordinating monetary and fiscal policy to simulate the centralization of policy characteristic of national economies. At the same time, the operation of such a monetary system must not prevent member countries from achieving what they view as important domestic goals. If it did frustrate such goals, secession from the monetary system and common market would likely occur by those members who believed themselves to be abused. Or, at the least, trade controls of one form or another would be imposed, which is tantamount to secession and disintegration. Indeed, the balance between these requirements is delicate. It is particularly difficult to achieve in the presence of nationalist aspirations by culturally, linguistically, and economically disparate member states. For these reasons, the more acceptable is the solution to the monetary problem provided by a system of flexible exchange rates.

The single-currency problem in the European Union remains basically unresolved. The political leadership in Germany believes that closer political union in Europe would make up for the loss of the German's beloved D-mark in 1999. German worries about giving up the D-mark have been rising as countries such as Spain and Italy strive to join the single currency.[2] As late as the end of 1996, the Germans still had not persuaded other countries, notably France, to accept a watertight "stability pact." The Germans want automatic significant fines to be levied on any single-currency country that borrows too much—defined as more than 3 percent of its Gross Domestic Product (GDP).

The likelihood that other countries in the European Union will accept the German proposal is not great. Most countries want the European Council of Ministers to exercise discretion over any fines, with a let-out if a country is ever in a mild recession. The reality of the German proposal leaves much to be desired. It's very unlikely indeed that a country that repeatedly defies its partners in the European Union by failing to control its deficits will readily hand over a large fine. Nevertheless, the Germans are insistent about securing at least the appearance of discipline—just as the British insist that they can bail out of the single-currency arrangement.

Certainly France and Germany are at odds over a single currency. The German Bundesbank in particular and Germans in general want the new euro to be as strong as the D-mark. They are nervous about how well the southern European members will manage fiscal affairs. They want assurance and thus the stability pact. The French, on the other hand, experiencing some stress under a strong franc, want a weak euro currency, particularly against the American dollar, so as to boost exports and retrieve lost jobs. Given the problems in Germany's economy and high unemployment rates, German businessmen may well agree with the French and a weaker euro. The likelihood of reaching the 1999 deadline for a single European currency may be unrealistic.

At the same time, Tory Eurosceptics in Great Britain continue their criticism over negotiations on a single currency. They were assured by the chancellor Kenneth Clarke that he had secured guarantees to protect an opted-out Britain. To be sure, the German-sponsored stability pact will apply to Great Britain if it ever chooses to opt into a single currency. Mr. Clarke supports the pact, on the basis that, whether British sterling currency is in or out, he wants the euro to be a sound currency that is not undermined by excessive borrowing.

And of course, as we noted, the political issue is whether a country that has deliberately ignored warnings that it is borrowing too much will actually pay a large fine to the European Community. The other and perhaps more important issue is the economic and monetary one, that is, once countries give up their monetary policy to a European central bank, how they will handle the inevitable shocks to their economies. This is all the more important because Europe has only limited labor mobility and thus far no general mechanism for making transfers from rich to poor countries. The instrument that may be available is fiscal policy that is constrained by the proposed stability pact.

The French are certainly alert to this problem, and so are reluctant to go along with the German stability proposal and fines for fiscal shortfalls. For their part, the British have not joined in to support the French position since they have opted out of the single-currency project. If the stability pact is indeed agreed upon, its rules may one day apply to Britain unless sterling never joins a single currency.

It is thus not surprising that the European Union under existing exchange rate arrangements has spent most of the period since the fall of the Berlin Wall in 1989 trying to strengthen links among the West European members instead of seriously reaching out to the postcommunist countries of the East, unnecessarily complicating easterners' transition to market democracy. This is what Professor Milton Friedman suggested years ago would likely be the case in the absence of a regime of flexible rates in the European Community. Free markets and exchange rates are more likely to be successful in promoting economic integration than a bureaucracy.

Clearly, economic integration is as important to East European stability as, say, NATO membership, and far less provocative to Moscow. The dissimilarity in economic arrangements existing in Eastern Europe (and, for that matter, elsewhere in the world) and the remainder of Europe can be better accommodated within a system of flexible exchange rates. The acquisition of East Germany into West Germany under a regime of a more or less fixed exchange rate has been shown to be a very expensive venture indeed. Other East European countries do not have a West German benefactor, even though West Germany appears to be the main champion of bringing in the East. Certainly Germany has a strong interest in the viability of its eastern neighbors, since that viability affects its own national security. Germans do not relish the idea that their eastern boundary may become the frontier between a "have" and a "have-not" Europe. There is also good reason to assume that Great Britain favors eastward expansion for the political and economic opportunities such expansion may provide.

Not everyone favors a German-oriented east. In particular, the Mediterranean countries—France, Italy, Greece, Portugal, and Spain—are less than enthusiastic about the opening toward the east. No doubt the concerns of these countries turn on the possibility of a reallocation in regional subsidies, competition for their towns, and a shift in the European Union's political center from the Mediterranean toward the German-oriented East. To this concern may also be added the possibility of neglect of the Mediterranean countries' own concerns about Islamic militants in nearby North Africa.

The extent to which the United States will participate in binding together a long-divided continent is an open question. The U.S. tilt toward Germany in the post–Cold War period and the Yugoslav catastrophe does not help reassure Mediterranean countries that German influence will not be dominant and their concerns over North Africa and Islam marginalized. Matters are not calmed on this score by the American tilt toward Turkey in spite of that country's sordid human rights record and growing Islamic influence. A more evenhanded approach by the United States would probably reassure these countries that their economies would not be slighted.

Adam Smith stated more than 200 years ago that the "invisible hand" of the free market produces many beneficial economic results. It may also produce certain beneficial political effects. Certainly changes in the global economy, which in good measure stem from integration of the world's economy, have also produced desirable political results. The collapse of the Soviet Union was a result of millions of people demanding free markets and participation in the world economy. The impact of the collapse continues to reverberate throughout the world.

It is not clear that if the European Union attempts to press its will on an increasingly diverse constituency, people and nations will fare better. Obviously, the idea is to find the right balance between the unique and personal identity of nations and the opportunities and demands of a larger entity, whether the European Union and/or the global economy. Yugoslavia and the Soviet Union are but examples where such a balance was not struck. The future may indeed hold other examples.

## A ROLE FOR THE EUROPEAN UNION

The problems are not likely to be easier for the European Union as well as the United States in their attempts to expand Europe and complete its integration. Flexible exchange rates, free markets, and prices are more likely to do so than a bureaucracy and expansion of NATO. In an insightful article, Thomas Friedman's advice is to "listen to the silence."[3] If we want to know what is wrong with NATO expansion, the key is to listen to the silence of Europeans on the subject. They neither talk much about nor indeed debate the issues involved. This is very strange, since it is they who are presumably threatened by the Russians. The reason for this, Thomas Friedman writes, is that the West Europeans think the real threat to them is not Russia, but Eastern Europe.

They see the threat as coming from these newly invited "market democracies," whose factories and farms want to export to Western

Europe at prices that will undercut the West Europeans and whose workers will migrate to Western Europe for jobs, which will drive down wages. It is, Friedman writes, Polish hams and Polish workers that are a clear and present danger to Western Europe, not Russian missiles and Russian tanks in some distant future.

For the Western Europeans, the easiest way to block Eastern European entry into the European Union is to offer them NATO expansion. This is, of course, a poor substitute for what the East Europeans really want and need. And in any case, the United States, it is assumed, will pay for NATO expansion and bring the Russians on board for such expansion. In short, the European Union assumes that the Americans will go along with this sham, argues Thomas Friedman.

NATO expansion is the second-term Clinton administration's first major foreign policy challenge. How such an expansion is to be carried out without undermining American arms-control treaties with Russia or the course of reform there, or even whether the benefits to the United States will be worth the price, no one has convincingly explained. None of this has been debated by the American public in Congress. To embroil America even further in the manifold troubles of East European countries never considered vital before the Berlin Wall fell surely merits serious debate.

The Clinton administration appears to be willing to be influenced by the interventionist ideas of the Munich mind-set of the 1930s in the fashion of generals fighting yesterday's wars. These ideas are a prescription for disaster for American foreign policy for the closing years of the twentieth century. It is a worldview logically incapable of establishing priorities for American action. Traditional internationalists, whether from the right or left, believe that aggression and turmoil anywhere in the world eventually will endanger America itself. Intervening in marginal regions obscures America's core needs, producing fuzzy political rationales, incoherent military policies, and ultimately public disillusionment within all international engagement. The results in former Yugoslavia (Bosnia and Croatia) and Somalia are but the more recent examples.

Naturally, supporters of interventionist foreign policy on the part of America dismiss the Powell Doctrine, which opposes the dispatch of American troops abroad except in overwhelming numbers for the most urgent reasons. Apparently, the Clinton administration is no longer wedded to it. The United States may be on the way to becoming the world's policeman, with all the consequences such a role produces. It is a role that sooner or later will cast in doubt America's world role and influence.

America has good reason not to glory in its wisdom nor its strength. Certainly we should exercise self-discipline and forsake armchair strategists fighting the wars of yesterday. The application of the lessons of Munich to Vietnam underscores the folly of the exercise. Misreading of the Yugoslav tragedy and failure to take evenhanded approach to all parties involved led the Clinton administration to permit the clandestine sale of weapons to the Bosnian Muslims by Iran and that country's foothold in a slice of Europe. The United States is now in an open-ended and prolonged commitment to peacekeeping in Bosnia and very likely beyond. While administration officials have defended the deployment of troops by citing the unstable and dangerous situation in Bosnia, military experts cite the same reasons for withdrawing troops.

The prospects for Bosnia and, for that matter, Tudjman's Croatia and Milosevic's Serbia are dim. For those who believed the military tasks of implementing the Dayton Peace Accords would be accomplished within a year, the results are indeed sobering. There is good reason to oppose new commitments to the region unless all parties to the dispute (Serbs, Croats, and Muslims) are treated fairly and in an evenhanded manner. The European Union should be willing to take on more of the burden, since it was Europe and its premature recognition of Slovenia, Croatia, and Bosnia that in good measure served to promote the tragedy of former Yugoslavia.

American dispatch of troops for purposes other than their assigned military tasks has drawn troops into tasks for they were unintended and thus endangered them. The hawks in Clinton's administration turned the humanitarian food mission in Somalia into a nation-building exercise, authorizing American forces to apprehend the warlord Mohammed Farah Aidid. As a result, a considerable number of American soldiers were killed in a region of no importance to America.

Many of the same hawks are now pushing with equal vigor that for American troops to take up the task of arresting those accused of war crimes in Bosnia. Placing combat-trained troops in a peacekeeping role with strict rules of engagement can make them argets of terrorist attacks, erode their fighting edge, and lower morale. Again Somalia, Lebanon, Saudi Arabia, and other less than hospitable places are ready examples.

There is the added problem that troops tied down in Bosnia for the stabilization force (SFOR), which replaced the international separation force (IFOR), impairs the ability of the United States to support a "two-war strategy" effectively (the ability to fight two major wars at the same time; Korea and the Persian Gulf are two areas often used as examples). This strategy had been a stated goal of the Clinton administration. To all of this may be added that less funding will be available for the Department of Defense training budget.

A Munich mind-set, or for that matter a Vietnam mind-set, are very poor guides to policy in the closing years of the twentieth century. Either worldview is logically incapable of establishing priorities for American action and would heighten the odds of the country plunging into an endless series of foreign trouble spots completely unrelated to its security and prosperity. Those leaders who applied the lessons of Munich to Vietnam learned to regret it. American involvement in the civil wars of such places as Korea, Vietnam, and Yugoslavia have been very unpleasant experiences indeed, for Americans and others. More than fifty ethnic and religious conflicts raging worldwide in the 1990s should sober even the most eager American interventionist.

The poor nations of Europe and their problems will continue to challenge the European Union. The collapse of communism reveals again a divided Europe. The division is between the have and have-not nations of Central and Eastern Europe.

The more prosperous and stable countries, such as Poland, Hungary, and the Czech Republic, are easing their way toward Western Europe and the European Union. Languishing to the south and east lie much poorer remnants of former Yugoslavia, Bulgaria, Romania, and Albania, where a legacy of communist rule, nationalist excesses, and reluctance to undertake market reforms have left faltering economies and political corruption. Indeed, even citizens with disposable resources that would permit them to travel abroad find themselves barred from visiting Western Europe, because their countries are on the European Union's "negative visa" list along with Zambia, Afghanistan, and other countries.[4]

Some observers predict that the European Union will extend its protective area around the old centers of Hapsburg Austria-Hungary, such as the Czech Republic, Hungary, and Poland. These countries have a common core of culture, religion, and experience with the countries of the European Union. They have also arranged (at least for the present) to put aside their worst nationalist instincts, with the promise of European Union reimbursement if they meet certain economic and democratic standards.

What happens to the rest of Europe is anyone's guess. It is this poor Europe that is desperately in need of assistance, especially from the European Union, if a division of Europe is to be avoided. This disparity should also focus American attention where America can really make a difference. Resources earmarked for NATO expansion could be used more productively by extending the scope of markets and democracy into the poorer half of Europe. Integration via private markets and prices is surely superior to integration through a reconfigured military organization such as NATO. Supporters of NATO react sharply to any criticism and note that a new European order requires a security framework and that NATO is the logical institution to provide it.

## NOTES

1.   See George Macesich, *Integration and Stabilization: A Monetary View* (Westport, CT: Praeger, 1996).

2.   See "European Union: Irish Mist," *The Economist* 341, no. 7995, December 7, 1996, p. 50.

3.   Thomas L. Friedman, "NATO or Tomato?" *New York Times*, Wednesday, January 22, 1997, p. A19. See also George F. Kennan, "A Fateful Error," *New York Times*, Wednesday, February 5, 1997, p. A19. In support of NATO expansion, see Madeleine Albright, "Enlarging NATO: Why Bigger Is Better," *The Economist* 342, no. 8004, February 15, 1997, pp. 21–23.

4.   See Jane Perlez, "New Bricks, Same Old Walls for Europe's Poor Nations," *New York Times*, Friday, January 24, 1997, pp. A1–A2.

# A New Political Economy Emerging?

## GROWING INFLUENCE OF THE AMERICAN MODEL

America's strong economic comeback during the 1990s is attributed to various factors. Some Europeans argue that America's strength owes much to a poorly paid and exploited labor force with which European countries cannot compete. Indeed, among many Europeans, there is a common belief that American workers live in near–Third World conditions, stuck in dead-end jobs and condemned to a steadily declining standard of living. This is the only explanation, in their view, for the large number of jobs created in the United States in the 1990s and the dramatic American industrial recovery that they thought would never happen.

The source of continuing surprise to many observers the world over is the ease with which the American economy reversed its decline and then outpaced a stagnant Europe to recover world markets that many people thought the United States had lost forever. Many observers were sure that America's day as an economic superpower was past. They were persuaded that the European Community and its member countries had definitely supplanted the United States. The European model of high wages and all-inclusive welfare protection had proved its superiority, not only in social, but also in economic terms.

When America rebounded, many analysts, especially Europeans, had to look elsewhere for an explanation of why they had been wrong. They found it soon enough in the view that American workers are exploited by a system in which the rewards of economic growth go exclusively to the rich. Contrary to American reality, the idea took hold that the new jobs created in the 1990s in the United States had been for McDonald's fast food and comparable unskilled, poorly paid occupations. Such studies as are readily available, however, indicate that more than 60 percent of new jobs created during the 1990s pay above-average wages. In real terms, American wages were approximately 10 percent higher in 1995 than they were in 1965.

For the Europeans and others, such data on American economic performance is largely ignored. European politicians can thus blame high unemployment and poor economic conditions not only on cheap Asian labor but also on cheap American labor. Trade union leaders, for their part, can and do argue that it is better to maintain high wages and expensive overall production costs, even if the result is widespread unemployment, than to follow the American model of alleged wage slavery.

The number of adherents to the American model, and its appealing performance is suggested by the fact that in 1996 more people live in a democracy than in a dictatorship. According to 1996 United Nations data, an estimated 3.1 billion people live in democracies and 2.66 billion do not. The biggest democracies are India, with 944.58 million, and the United States, with 269.44 million. On the other side are China, with 1.232 billion, and Indonesia, with 200.453 million. The pendulum has swung sharply in favor of the democratic nations in the last few years, owing largely to the 280 million people in the nations that comprised the former Soviet Union.

Given the performance record for the American model, its appeal for many people is understandable. It is likely that the model may serve as the key to the new political economy that is emerging in the world. The nearest competitors to the American model are the market-oriented capitalist models in Europe and Japan. All these models show certain characteristics, such as private enterprise, private ownership, and reliance on the market mechanism to allocate resources. There are, however, important differences that may well limit their influence and/or adoption. Thus, the American model focuses on individual action as opposed to collective action, which is stressed by the other two. The European model includes a more diverse cultural mix than either the model of Japan or that of America.

Consider these three models. In the American model, the emphasis is placed on the individual, market, and competition. Wealth accumulation and consumption are emphasized. Little if any class resentment is incorporated in the American model. In fact, the self-made millionaires are considered role models for others to follow. Competition is the American model for promoting efficiency, providing for consumer wants, and encouraging innovation.

The American model is deeply embedded in the individualism of the nineteenth century. In many respects, the opening of the American West and the flow of immigrants from Europe, many fleeing government oppression and economic hardship, promoted and raised individualism to a very high level. The United States was viewed as a land of opportunity where an individual had a chance to get ahead through individual effort. It was expected, moreover, that each generation would be better off than its predecessor. This is, in essence, the American dream.

Government presence and intervention in the American economy was present from the beginning. The federal government, from the beginning in 1787, promoted industry and commerce through tariff laws, subsidies, and other measures. In the nineteenth century, government attention focused on regulatory control on various forms of anticompetitive business practices, including price-fixing and division of markets. By the 1930s and the Great Depression, government activity in the economy increased significantly. Various social and security nets were put in place for the population, and regulatory agencies were created to regulate banks, securities markets, and communication. During the World War II years and the years of the Cold War, government intervention increased significantly, as discussed earlier in this study.

## THE EUROPEAN MODEL

### Historical Perspective

The European model in many respects is older than its American counterpart and evolved under different conditions. Although capitalism has its roots in Europe, many of the leading economists and their ideas have had greater impact in the United States than in Europe. The writings of Adam Smith, David Ricardo, John Stuart Mill, and others provided the foundations for free-market capitalism and are important elements in the American model.

European socialist parties of both the non-Marxist and Marxist variety were formed and gained strength from the middle of the nineteenth century. In many European countries, socialist parties are important political organizations with considerable influence in society and government. The parties are committed to raising wages and improving working conditions of workers. Government intervention has increased in many European countries since the closing years of the nineteenth century. This intervention has taken the form of various social and economic measures aimed at improving the conditions of workers. Two world wars and a depression further served to strengthen government intervention in Europe, as they did in the United States.

In the European model, the essentials of capitalism do exist. The profit motive, private property ownership, and private enterprise are all present. The difference between the American model and the European model is that in the former the emphasis is placed on individual action, while in the latter, the emphasis is on collective action. Moreover, the European model includes more countries and so is more diverse than its American counterpart. The common threads in the various European countries are the elaborate system of social welfare benefits, such as health, pensions, and unemployment, and training measures designed to serve the population. In fact, every aspect of economic activity in Europe carries with it some form of government measure. Government-mandated benefits in Europe are more prevalent than in the United States.

The role of government in the European model is not limited simply to providing social welfare benefits. Governments have been involved in other ways. In many European countries, state intervention goes back to the 1500s (if indeed not earlier), when nationalism and economics were combined in a close nexus in these countries and their overseas dependencies.[1] The body of loosely knit ideas and practices we now call "mercantilism," or economic nationalism, developed and eclipsed gradually but not completely, as testified in the legislative practices of modern nations. Mercantilism is the economic counterpart of political nationalism, and nationalism itself is a force in the development of nation-states. England, Spain, and France became nation-states rather early; Italy, Germany, and other Continental nation-states emerged relatively late.

Most studies date English mercantilism from the end of the Wars of the Roses and the beginning of the reign of King Henry VII in 1485, though scattered evidence suggests a much earlier date. Mercantilism peaked in Queen Elizabeth's reign in the late 1500s and through the Stuart period in the 1600s. Much of the English mercantilist legislation was not removed from the books until the midnineteenth century, though many of the laws had not been enforced for years. In Spain mercantilism was in full bloom during the 1500s and 1600s. It peaked in France during the ministry of Colbert in the latter 1600s.

A characteristic of mercantilist policies that distinguished them from the earlier medieval policies is that they tended to tax imports and provide subsidies to exports. Earlier the tendency was to tax both imports and exports. Mercantilist policies, in effect, turned from goods to money, to the increase in the stock of money, and to encouragement of exports and discouragement of imports. In this manner, the producer was helped at the expense of the consumer. To be sure, even at the height of mercantilism, the interests of the producers were not always dominant. Thus the English Corn Laws had the consumer in mind as well as the producer; as indeed did the Statute of Monopolies, which was designed to protect the consumer form the more obvious damages brought about producer interests.

Many laws designed to protect the producer also have domestic employment as their goal. Domestic employment and development of home industry were the stated goals of duties imposed, for instance, against English cloth by the French and Swedish governments in the mid-1660s.

The emigration of artisans was of considerable concern to nation-states. Laws discouraging such movement were on the books of most countries during the mercantilist period. Indeed, in 1719 the British government prohibited the emigration of skilled workers, though the law itself was evaded. Patents and monopolies were extended to foreigners to entice them to settle and develop new industries. Machinery, on the other hand, was not to be exported, nor indeed were drawings of such machinery.

Sea power played an important role in the mercantilist scheme of things, so shipping and ships were very important. Exports were to be carried in domestic ships. Explorations and colonies were encouraged and trading opportunities cultivated. The objective was to make the home country the focus of an empire, with the wealth and power that such a position commanded.

In England laws encouraged colonial as well as British shipping. Indeed it was not until the middle of the nineteenth century that British navigation laws were repealed. Along with the policy of protecting domestic manufacturers, those in the colonies were repressed. Such action in the colonies generated protests and other disturbances, including open revolution in the British American colonies, which subsequently became the United States and the "American model."

In France during the ministry of Jean-Baptiste Colbert (1619–1683), mercantilist policy reached a peak. Government service was refocused and improved. Industry was regulated in considerable detail. Companies were established to trade with America and India. Restrictions were imposed on the emigration of artisans and craftsmen. The merchant marine and navy were expanded and strengthened.

Spain, whose explorers and soldiers in South America sent to the home country vast quantities of precious metals, was viewed with envy and fear by the other growing nation-states. Indeed, the growing economic and naval power of Spain prompted England to undertake measures in self-defense. Spain was later displaced in English eyes as a threat by Holland and France in the 1600s and 1700s.

Policies in Spain were decidedly of mercantilist flavor. Laws forbade exports in foreign ships when Spanish ships were available. In fact, sea trade was very closely controlled, in good measure for defense purposes. Domestic industry was protected. Gold and silver were not to be exported, even though Spanish trade was in fact distributing the precious metals throughout Europe.

In sum, mercantilist policies focused on building national strength, even at the expense of individual welfare and wealth. The state and not necessarily the individual formed the foundations upon which policies and laws were based. Wealth, in this view, was not maximized by free private individual enterprise. Indeed, mercantilist policies did not view as correct the maximization of individual wealth, within the nation and through it the achievement of national wealth, as Adam Smith argues in *The Wealth of Nations*. Mercantilist policies can better be interpreted as placing on a national basis the medieval policies that focused on regulation, whose aim was to achieve a balance among various classes of people with a modicum of justice for all.

The principles and policies of mercantilism have been challenged repeatedly. They have, nonetheless, never been completely repudiated in the legislative halls of nation-states. On the contrary, these principles and policies maintain a remarkable vitality, as the several models under wider review in this study indicates.

Nevertheless, the seeds of individual liberty were at work even in the mercantilist world. The emerging middle class ceased to support absolutism when it ceased to serve its commercial interests, particularly in such matters as property rights. Even Machiavelli and Bodin counseled against the taking of private property by the sovereign without just cause. It was precisely at this point that absolute monarchy broke down. It simply was not wise enough to incorporate such advice into its program of action when dealing with the rights of property.

The issue of property rights coalesced with issues of religious freedom and popular rights, the middle class making up the bulk of support for such rights. The assault upon the absolute monarchy, prompted by religious groups demanding toleration, quickly gathered in support others to whom the freedom of conscience appealed and ultimately won their participation in the defense of property rights. To be sure, the toleration of those groups for the rights of others left much to be desired. When their own rights were threatened, however, they were very strenuous indeed in their defense. Most of the arguments came from the dissenting Protestant groups, but when Catholics sensed their own rights in jeopardy, they waxed eloquent against despotism. Indeed, two of the greatest defenses of popular sovereignty were written by the Spanish Jesuits Mariana and Suarez.

It was Machiavelli's principles, however, that rising national states adopted almost to the letter. These called for freedom from all superior codes or laws whatsoever. In those precepts Machiavelli followed the example of the Papacy, which was sovereign as no other state. Though theoretically bound by natural law, the pope could dispense with violations of it. Faith need not be kept with heretics, as the Council of Constance had decreed in its dealings with Jan Hus. Machiavelli read "state" for "church" and "enemy" for "heretic" and founded the modern religion of the state.

### Intellectual Roots

For many years Great Britain, in which the classical school of economics emerged and grew, was much more advanced than the continents of Europe and America. Thanks in part to its geography, which afforded it a measure of security, Britain, unlike other countries in Europe, was able to develop a modern industrial base relatively early. Earlier mercantilist policies undoubtedly also helped to channel resources to prepare the foundation for Europe's industrial advance. And when to this is added the available human and natural resources as well as an individualistic philosophy and political democracy, it seems only to be expected that Britain would have been able to push ahead of other nations in industrial and economic development.

In much of Europe, on the other hand, large estates remained important. Governments were absolute monarchies, unlike the limited monarchy of Britain. Excesses of the French Revolution gave new strength to a more conservative outlook. It is thus not surprising that philosophical, political, and economic thought differed markedly from the individualist philosophy upon which British classical economics was based. To Adam Smith, *The Wealth of Nations* was the sum of individual wealth and the nation only an aggregation of individuals. Government functions were to be limited to providing primarily defense and justice.

The European Continental school viewed these issues very differently. It was strongly influenced by the so-called Romantic movement, which can be described as a revolt against the material and logical in favor of the search for the inner spirit and truth of nature and man. German nationalism was one of the "truths" that focused its expression in the writings of such Romanticists as Fichte, Hegel, Muller, and List. Acceptance of the ideas encompassed in the Romantic movement led by A. H. Muller (1779–1829) and Friedrich List (1789–1846) amounted to criticizing the position of Adam Smith and the classical school.

What was the role of the individual in society as viewed by the Romanticists? It differed sharply from that of John Locke, Adam Smith, and their followers. Jean-Jacques Rousseau (1712–1778) considered the general will or objective of society to be distinct from that of the individual. Montesquieu, in search for a theory of law, found it in the spirit of society to which the law applied. Government cannot rule arbitrarily, according to Montesquieu. It must rule in the spirit of the society. To Immanuel Kant (1724–1804) in Germany, the concept of duty was important. Men can be free, but being free, they have a duty to other men. Other Germans, such as Johann G. Fichte (1762–1814) and Georg Wilhelm Hegel (1770–1831), went further than Kant. Fichte envisioned a moral will behind the individual will—a purpose of the universe, or God, whose will projected itself into individual wills. Hegel in turn developed this concept into a comprehensive view of history, society, and philosophy.

Consider briefly Hegel's philosophy. To Hegel the entire universe was a manifestation of God, or the absolute. Its primary purpose was revealed in the human mind. History was the unfolding of this purpose in the external phenomena over time. Human social organization and its changes were reflected in the evolving ideas in the minds of men, through which they sought the will of God. Advancement was attained through a series of struggles between ideas seeking the final truth. This is the familiar Hegelian thesis, or theory, clashing with its antithesis, or objection, and emerging finally as a synthesis or solution. Through this struggle, man and his institutions are seen as becoming more perfect and more consistent with the ideal.

According to the Hegelian view, man's nature was not to be found in Locke's explanation. Man's nature was not a bundle of wants whose satisfaction was sought. His purpose was to be achieved through the harmonious development of all his faculties not only for himself, but for society as a whole. True freedom was expressed in association with others in society, including the state itself. A person who had achieved this freedom would espouse social wants. In effect, his wants were for the things that were for the social good as well. A concept of freedom that involved conflict between individual freedom and society was simply a manifestation of social and ethical immaturity.

To reach the Hegelian ideal, an individual must find his place in society and his will or purpose must become the social purpose or social will. To Hegel, existing institutions were to be accepted and used, since the true good was achievable within their framework. Hegel's writings are all the more important since they spanned a good part of the revolutionary upheaval and reaction in Europe.

On this score it is also important to note that Marx's social philosophy was also Hegelian in that he accepted Hegel's concept of the wholeness of society as well as his belief that human evolution is to be interpreted as progress toward a goal or ideal. Marx, however, also rejected in an important sense Hegelian philosophy. Unlike Hegel, who underscored the evolution of ideas and perceived the outward phenomena of society as reflecting the progress of ideas, Marx emphasized the outward. According to Marx, the course of development of human ideas and social organization was influenced by external and particularly economic factors.

The Continental views on property and money are particularly restrictive. Rousseau's opposition to property rights as they existed in

France are well known. He considered the system in France of his time an outrage against the rights of man. He too, like Locke, based his property rights theory on the idea of natural rights. Unlike Locke, who used natural rights to justify property rights, Rousseau used natural rights doctrine to condemn the practice of property rights.

This does not deny Hegel's later view that property rights are integral elements in individual and social development. Rousseau simply underscored the point that in the France of his time many men were excluded from participating in the exercise of property rights. Many were excluded in Hegel's Germany when he wrote. The reason for this difference evidently was that Hegel, unlike Rousseau, chose to ignore the reality of the situation.

To Kant, property rights were subject to government consent, since individual property rights affected others in society. The government represented these others, and thus these rights were within its proper domain. Nevertheless, individual property rights were to be defended on the principle that justice was achieved through inequality of property. They represented rewards to the individual for his contribution to society.

Fichte's and Smith's views on government underscored the differences between the classical and Continental schools of thought. According to Smith, government activity should restrict itself to defense, justice, and certain public works that by their nature had to be undertaken collectively. It is this third item that could be and indeed is interpreted as a call for a large amount of activity by government. After all, there are many projects without prospects of profit to individuals, with social benefits in excess of their social costs. This could amount to a considerable size in the "output mix" for a government—far larger, undoubtedly, than what Adam Smith had in mind for government.

Fichte, on the other hand, viewed government as a body with members or organs. It was more than an assembly of individuals as viewed by Smith and Locke. Government was a composite whole in much the same fashion as a human body is composed of its constituent elements. Thus it is that the state could not be viewed, according to Fichte, as a simple assemblage of individuals, any more than could the human body be considered a collection of cells. In effect, Fichte's output mix for government was more comprehensive and encompassing that of Smith.

On property rights, Fichte argued that an individual possessed such property rights as were useful for the necessities of the state. In effect, the individual was to agree to use the property suitably and usefully for the necessities of the state. If he purchased farm lands, for instance, he had to cultivate these lands. Property rights were also extended to profession, provided the individual supplied work of sufficient quantity and quality. Thus the links between property rights and social duties were clearly established.

These links between property rights and social duties extend back into the medieval ages and the European guilds and forward into their modern counterparts in Fascist Italy and Nazi Germany. In less extreme form, they also exist in the contemporary system of professional organizations throughout the world. In various manpower planning schemes within central planning organizations there is also a modern counterpart to Fichte's argument that it was the responsibility of the government or its designated bodies to ascertain the manpower requirements of the various branches of the economy. These views are in marked contrast to the individualistic rights argued by Locke and Smith.

Indeed, Hegel's view of property underscored the fact that like other rights, property rights were subject to the sovereignty of the state. It was more than individual possession, according to Hegel. It was an expression of personality. In its possession a person became rational. Since the expression of personality through property was beneficial, the state protected it. Moreover, Hegel argued in favor of inequality of property because among persons variously endowed, inequality must occur and equality would be wrong. Justice demanded merely, according to Hegel, that every person should have property, not that every man's property should be equal.

Fichte's view on money, again, contrasted with those of Adam Smith, David Ricardo, and others of the classical school. Money was something more than a means to facilitate exchange. It represented, according to Fichte, a state recognition of its indebtedness to private cash balance holders. Unlike Ricardo, for instance, Fichte did not believe the state could overissue money. He did not view a general rise in prices as having distributional effects. Many of Fichte's views were later incorporated by George Friedrich Knapp (1842–1926) into his work on money. This view of money was also supported by Friedrich von Gentz (1764–1832) and Adam Heinrich Muller (1779–1829).

Though sympathetic to some of Smith's views, Muller did not agree with Smith's materialism. He was much more favorably disposed to the views of Hegel and Fichte on the state and society as constituting a whole.

The individual was part of society, in which regard for others was a critical element. Indeed, like Hegel and Fichte, Muller appeared to glorify the political nation-state. It does appear that Hegel, Fichte, and particularly Muller were the ideological forebear of German National Socialism.

For his part, Gentz also appeared to defend feudalism, which was still prevalent in many German states at the beginning of the nineteenth century. Feudalism did not recognize complete property ownership but only rights and associated duties. Thus, it fit well into the ideological concept of an organic society. To Muller personal goods were of the same gender. They invalued rights and duties to others. The individual thus was not completely his own person, since he also had duties to others. Production was important because the supply of goods and services were increased as a result. Muller, however, did more. He included as factors of production the nation's entire spectrum of ideas and culture capital.

In essence, Gentz, Muller, and others in the Continental European school supported the Fichte-Hegel view of society in much the same fashion as Adam Smith produced the economic counterpart of the philosophical individualism of John Locke. There are other important differences between the classical and Continental schools. Consider the issue of economic nationalism and protectionism.

Friedrich List (1789–1846) was certainly among the more important contributors to the discussions of economic nationalism and protectionism. He argued that the economics of Smith and his followers totally ignored the nation-state and its requirements. According to List, societies passed through several historical stages. There was, first, the barbarian or primitive stage. This was followed by the second or pastoral stage. In the third stage, a society became self-sufficient in agriculture. The fourth included agriculture as well as manufacturers for local consumption. The fifth stage included agriculture as well as manufacturers for world trade.

According to List, the free-trade policies advocated by Smith and the classical school were suitable only for countries in the fifth stage. In List's view, such an arrangement was suitable only to Great Britain but not to Germany or the United States. Both countries needed to expand their manufacturers in order to reach the stage of development that Great Britain had already achieved. The problem, which is not addressed by Smith and his policy or policies is that each nation must pursue to make progress in their various stages of development. In a completely unified world body of nations, List argued, economic interdependence and specialization could be defended. In reality, however, the possibilities of war and/or interruption of trade among nations was ever present. Moreover, any nation with only agriculture as its industry was depriving itself of the full productivity and output of all its resources.

The policies recommended by List to achieve and develop manufacturers in such countries as Germany called for import tariffs to be imposed gradually and with care on desired industries so as not to be disruptive to the economy. These duties were to be lowered as the industry in question achieved the necessary maturity to compete. The policies were to be appropriately synchronized to the stage of a country's development.

The economics of the classical school did not have an enthusiastic following on the continent. The Europeans and now some Americans tended to prefer the protectionist policies advocated by such writers on political economy as List. Others incorporated what they considered the relevant features of the classical school of economics into a broader study of an integrated and evolving society. The philosophical background for this evolutionary view of economics was provided by Hegel. This was the so-called German historical school of economics, which prevailed on the continent between 1843 and 1883. Dominant figures in this school included Wilhelm Friedrich Roscher (1817–1894), Bruno Hilderbrand (1812–1878), Karl Gustav Adolph Knies (1821–1898), Gustav von Schmoller (1838–1917), and Karl Bucher (1847–1930).

According to the German historical school, economic organization and theory must be related to the environment. In this view, classical economics is not of universal application; it is limited to the society in which it emerged. An economics of general applications must incorporate a study of the history of various societies and human society as a whole, and such a study must be inductive. Principles are to be formed by examining data concerning the environment to which they could be considered to apply. These studies are to be undertaken by economists together with historians and statisticians. Ironically, Adam Smith's *Wealth of Nations* is surely consistent with the objectives and desires of the German historical school, while the works of David Ricardo and Nassau Senior (1790–1864) are not.

In particular, those of the historical school disagree with the view of the classical school that enlightened self-interest is the primary economic motive. They argue that human nature is much more complex, so that reasoning based on self-interest is not of general application.

This is the intellectual and historical environment in which the European model evolved into its present form. Government support for industry and intervention in the economy continues. A case in point is Airbus Industries, an aircraft industry owned by the governments of France, Germany, Spain, and Great Britain that is designed to get Europe back into civilian aviation production. Although privatization of state-owned firms has been occurring in all European countries, state-owned firms account for an important part of GNP in such countries as France, Spain, and Italy.

It is generally agreed that Germany is the representative country in the European model. For all its postwar success, Germany now faces the challenges of globalization. Indeed, the challenges facing Germany are a microcosm of those facing Europe. A strong euro currency and macroeconomic stability may not be sufficient in themselves. It appears that structural reforms are essential. Demographic changes in Germany and in Europe require a restructuring of social security systems and more flexible labor markets if the challenges of globalization are to be met. Labor market rigidities are impeding adjustment and driving up unemployment, which in Germany in the first half of 1997 registered more than 12 percent.

If the monetary union is achieved, the problem of unemployment may well be intensified, not only in Germany, but elsewhere in Europe as well, since exchange rate changes would no longer provide a means for dealing with excessive wage increases or other disturbances. In the absence of a flexible labor market, pockets of high unemployment could result, with unwelcome fiscal and social effects that in turn could promote the growth of protectionism and undermine the prospects that the European Union would be able to create a financial system that is as deep and efficient as that of the United States.

## THE STATE-DIRECTED MODEL OF JAPAN IN RETROSPECT

Japan was the last of the major economies to industrialize. Its model is now more unique than the other two. The country was insulated from foreign influence for much of its history. When the country finally turned to the West in the midnineteenth century, the state assumed a dominant role in directing and guiding economic development. The government supplied part of the capital needed for business either directly or through the medium of special banks that continue to exist today. I have discussed elsewhere in this study the unique nature of the Japanese model and its problems.

Suffice it at this point to underscore the need for reform so as to make the Japanese economy more flexible and therefore capable of dealing with the exchanges of globalization. Even in so fundamental an issue as the operation of the country's central bank, the Finance Ministry has excessive influence. The finance minister, for example, has the power to order central bank policy changes and the power to fire central bank personnel. Indeed, critics blame what they call the Finance Ministry's excessive influence over the central bank for the low interest rates of the 1980s that fed an overheated economy which collapsed in the 1990s.

Reforms applied to freeing the economy are crucial. This means deregulation rather than the broad, administrative reforms that are pushed. The Japanese model would be more attractive if its bureaucrats had less discretion and were more accountable to their political and electoral clients.

The push for reform in Japan and elsewhere may get assistance. The newly formed World Trade Organization (WTO) is now apparently empowered to go inside the borders of seventy countries that signed it to review how quickly and effectively they are deregulating key parts of their economies. That includes assessing whether they are following through on their commitments to allow foreigners to invest in businesses that countries from France to Japan to Singapore have long reserved for government-run monopolies. And if the WTO finds evidence of foot-dragging, it can, in theory at least, authorize penalties.[2]

## NOTES

1.    See George Macesich, *Economic Nationalism and Stability* (New York: Praeger, 1985).

2.    See David E. Sanger, "Playing the Trade Card: U.S. Is Exporting its Free-Market Values through Global Commercial Agreements," *New York Times*, Monday, February 17, 1997, pp. 1, 27.

# Bibliography

## CHAPTER 1

Blaug, Mark. "Kuhn versus Lakatos, or Paradigm versus Research Programmes in the History of Economics." In *Paradigms and Revolutions*, ed. Gary Gutting. Notre Dame, IN: University of Notre Dame Press, 1980, pp. 137–59.

Brunner, Karl. "The 1976 Nobel Prize in Economics." *Science*, November 5, 1976, p. 648.

Friedman, Milton. "Monetary Policy: Theory and Practice." *Journal of Money, Credit, and Banking* (February 1982), p. 101.

Hayek, F. A. *The Constitution of Liberty*. Chicago: University of Chicago Press, 1960.

Johnson, Harry. "The Nobel Milton." *The Economist*, October 23, 1976, p. 95.

Kuhn, Thomas S. *The Structure of Scientific Revolutions*. Second edition, enlarged. Chicago: University of Chicago Press, 1970.

Macesich, George. *Monetarism: Theory and Policy*. New York: Praeger, 1983.

Vickers, D. *Studies in the Theory of Money, 1690–1776*. Philadelphia: Chilton, 1959.

## CHAPTER 2

Bailey, Martin J. "Administered Prices and Inflation." In U.S. Congress, Joint Economic Committee, *The Relationship of Prices to Economic Stability and Growth, Compendium*, March 1958.

Cagan, Phillip. "The Monetary Dynamics of Hyperinflation." In *Studies in the Quantity Theory of Money*, ed. Milton Friedman. Chicago: University of Chicago Press, 1956, pp. 25–117.

Friedman, Milton. "Current Critical Issues in Wage Theory and Prices." In *Proceedings of the Eleventh Annual Meeting*, Industrial Relations Research Association, Chicago, 1959.

———. "Government Revenue from Inflation." *Journal of Political Economy* (July/August 1971), pp. 852–54.

———. "The Role of Monetary Policy." *American Economic Review* 58 (March 1968), pp. 1–17.

Macesich, George. *Monetarism: Theory and Policy*. New York: Praeger, 1983, pp. 139–58.

Rees, Albert. "Do Unions Cause Inflation?" *Journal of Law and Economics* (October 1959), pp. 84–94.


## CHAPTER 3

Angell, James W. "Appropriate Monetary Policy and Operations in the United States Today." *Review of Economics and Statistics* 42 (August 1960), pp. 247–52.

Bronfenbrenner, Martin. "Monetary Rules: A New Look." *Journal of Law and Economics* 8 (October 1965), pp. 173–94.

Fisher, Irving. *Stabilizing the Dollar*. New York: Macmillan, 1920.

Friedman, Milton. "Commodity-Reserve Currency." *Journal of Political Economy* 59 (June 1951), pp. 203–32. Reprinted in Milton Friedman, ed., *Essays in Positive Economics*. Chicago: University of Chicago Press, 1953, pp. 204–50.

———. "A Monetary and Fiscal Framework for Economic Stability." In *Essays in Positive Economics*, ed. Milton Friedman. Chicago: University of Chicago Press, 1953, pp. 133–56.

———. *The Optimal Quantity of Money and Other Essays*. Chicago: Aldine, 1969.

———. *A Program for Monetary Stability*. The Millar Lectures, No. 3. New York: Fordham University Press, 1968.

———. "The Role of Monetary Policy." *American Economic Review* 58 (March 1968), p. 17.

Friedman, Milton, and Anna J. Schwartz. *A Monetary History of the United States*. Princeton: Princeton University Press, 1963.

Gramley, Lyle E. "Guidelines for Monetary Policy: The Case Against Simple Rules." In *Readings in Money, National Income, and Stabilization Policy*, revised, ed. W. L. Smith and R. L. Teigan. Homewood, IL: Irwin, 1970, pp. 488–93.

Hart, Albert G. "The Chicago Plan for Banking Reform." *Review of Economic Studies* 2 (1935), pp. 104–16.

Mints, Lloyd W. "Monetary Policy and Stabilization." *American Economic Review Papers and Proceedings* 41 (May 1951), pp. 188–93.

———. *Monetary Policy for a Competitive Society.* New York: McGraw-Hill, 1950.

"Monetary Policy Mysteries." *The Economist* 7985, September 28, 1996, p. 96.

*Report to the Congress of the Commission on the Role of Gold in the Domestic and International Monetary System,* vols. 1 and 2. Washington, DC: The Secretary of the Treasury, March 1982.

Schwartz, Anna J. "Introduction." In *A Retrospective on the Classical Gold Standard, 1821–1931,* ed. Michael D. Bordo and Anna J. Schwartz. Chicago: University of Chicago Press, 1984, pp. 1–20.

Selden, Richard T. "Stable Monetary Growth." In U.S. Congress, House Committee on Banking and Currency, *Compendium on Monetary Policy Guidelines and Federal Reserve Structure.* Pursuant to H.R. 11. Subcommittee on Domestic Finance of the Committee on Banking and Currency, House of Representatives, 90th Cong., 2d sess., 1968.

Shaw, Edward S. "Monetary Stability in a Growing Economy." In *The Allocation of Economic Resources: Essays in Honor of B. F. Haley.* ed. Edward S. Shaw. Stanford: Stanford University Press, 1959, pp. 218–35.

Simons, Henry C. "A Positive Program for Laissez-Faire: Some Proposals for a Liberal Economic Policy." In *Public Policy Pamphlet* 15, ed. H. D. Gideonse. Chicago: University of Chicago Press, 1934.

———. "Rules versus Authorities in Monetary Policy." *Journal of Political Economy* 4 (February 1936), pp. 1–30.

Snyder, Carl. "The Problem of Monetary and Economic Stability." *Quarterly Journal of Economics* 49 (February 1935), p. 198.

U.S. Congress. House Committee on Banking and Currency. *Stabilization, Hearings* before Committee on Banking and Currency. Stabilization Hearings, House of Representatives on H.R. 11806, 7th Cong., 1st sess., 1928.

U.S. Congress. Senate Committee on Banking and Currency. *Restoring and Maintaining the Average Purchasing Power of the Dollar,* Hearings before Committee on Banking and Currency. Senate on H.R. 11499 and S. 4429, 72d Cong., 1st sess., 1932.

Warburton, Clark. "Rules and Implements of Monetary Policy." *Journal of Finance* 8 (March 1953), pp. 1–21.

———. "The Volume of Money and Price Lead Between the World Wars." *Journal of Political Economy* 53 (1945), pp. 150–63.

Whittlesey, Charles R. "Rules, Discretion, and Central Bankers." In *Essays in Money and Banking in Honour of Richard S. Sayers,* ed. C. R. Whittlesey and J. S. Wilson. London: Oxford University Press, 1968, pp. 252–65.

## CHAPTER 4

Huntington, Samuel. "Cultural Explanations." *The Economist* 341, November 9, 1996, no. 7991, pp. 23–26.
Haas, Richard N. "It's Dangerous to Disarm: The U.S. Needs Its Nuclear Arsenal." *New York Times*, Wednesday, December 11, 1996, p. A21.
Kennedy, Paul. *The Rise and Fall of Great Powers*. New York: Random House, 1988.
Macesich, George. *Transformation and Emerging Markets*. Westport, CT: Praeger, 1996.

## CHAPTER 5

Arkoun, Mohammed. *Common Question, Uncommon Answers*. Translated and edited by Robert D. Lee, Boulder, CO: Westview Press, 1994.
"The Backlash in Latin America." *The Economist* 341, November 30, 1996, no. 7994, pp. 19–21.
Bohlen, Celestine. "A Marxist Splinter Party Maintains Influence in Italy." *New York Times*, Tuesday, December 17, 1996, p. A6.
Macesich, George. *Transformation and Emerging Markets* (Westport, CT: Praeger, 1996).
Milapidus, Ira. "Islam without Militance." *New York Times Book Review*, August 21, 1996, pp. A9–10.
_____. "Tigers or Tortoises?" *The Economist* 341, October 26, 1996, no. 7989, p. 98.

## CHAPTER 6

Hagen, Everett E. *On the Theory of Social Change*. Homewood, IL: The Dorsey Press, 1962.
Kuznets, Simon. *Modern Economic Growth: Rate, Structure and Spread*. New Haven: Yale University Press, 1967.
Rostow, W. W. *The Stages of Economic Growth*. Cambridge, England: Cambridge University Press, 1960.

## CHAPTER 7

Albright, Madeleine. "Enlarging NATO: Why Bigger Is Better." *The Economist* 342, no. 8004, February 15, 1997, pp. 21–23.
European Union: Irish Mist." *The Economist* 341, no. 7995, December 7, 1996, p. 50.
Friedman, Thomas L. "NATO or Tomato?" *New York Times*, Wednesday, January 22, 1997, p. A19.

Kennan, George F. "A Fateful Error." *New York Times*, Wednesday, February 5,
    1997, p. A19.
Macesich, George. *Integration and Stabilization: A Monetary View.* Westport,
    CT: Praeger, 1996.
Perlez, Jane. "New Bricks, Same Old Walls for Europe's Poor Nations." *New
    York Times*, Friday, January 24, 1997, pp. A1–A2.

## CHAPTER 8

Macesich, George. *Economic Nationalism and Stability.* New York: Praeger,
    1985.
Sanger, David E. "Playing the Trade Card: U.S. Is Exporting its Free-Market
    Values through Global Commercial Agreements." *New York Times*,
    Monday, February 17, 1997, pp. 1, 27.

# Index

**About the Author**

GEORGE MACESICH is Professor of Economics at Florida State University. His most recent books include *Integration and Stabilization: A Monetary View* (Praeger, 1996) and *Monetary Reform in Former Socialist Economies* (Praeger, 1994).